I0763423

STAND OUT

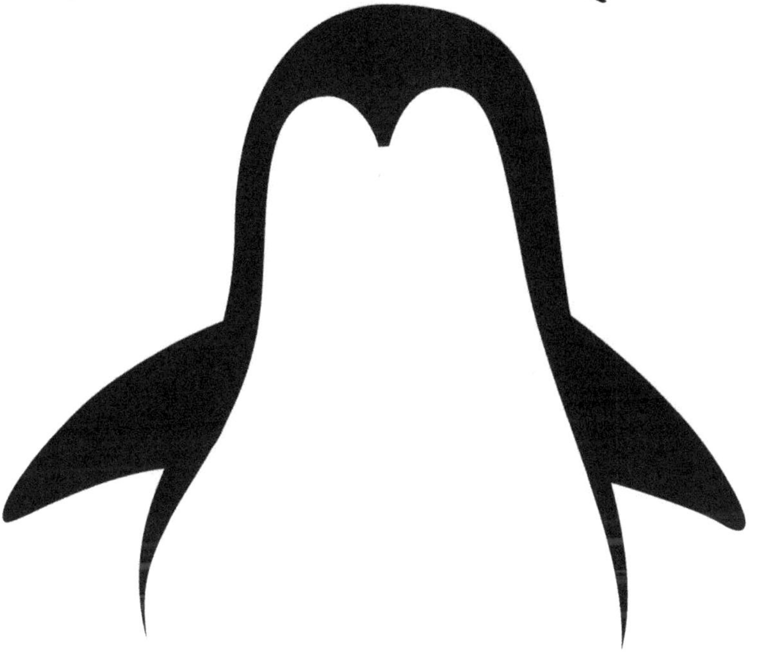

THE BEST OF THE RED PENGUIN COLLECTION
VOLUME 1
AN ANTHOLOGY EDITED BY JK LARKIN

Stand Out

Published by Red Penguin Books

Bellerose Village, New York

Library of Congress Control Number: 2021900673

ISBN

Print 978-1-63777-008-5 / 978-1-63777-014-6

Digital 978-1-63777-013-9

Contents

PART I

Realiteen: Reflecting On Growing Up

Realiteen: Reflections On Growing Up is a celebration of what it means to be a teenager. Through the stories of our diverse cast of authors, this anthology represents how this pivotal age has come to mean so much more than the seven years by which it is defined. Read a collection of experiences that capture the essence of what it means to find oneself along the path from child to adult. Perhaps you might even find yourself reflecting on your own memories of young adulthood!

1

The Topography of My Chest

EVELYN SHARENOV

I found out later it was the superintendent who discovered the hard, ugly lump glued into his wife's small breast. It was the same night she conceived their tenth child. "Goyim," my mother said. She shook her head when she heard that Estelle was pregnant again.

Most of the families in our neighborhood had a couple of kids. Some of their parents had numbers tattooed on their wrists and were on their second families. Then there were the outliers – the occasional childless couple, objects of pity. The superintendent and Estelle did their Catholic duty. My mother looked down her nose at them. She walked through our lives with her head in a miasma of superiority.

The superintendent didn't tell his wife about the lump. I guessed she wasn't a woman who would touch her own breasts. He wept in secret, swiped at his eyes as he pushed his wide broom or sloshing mop up and down the tile floors of the apartment building. I imagined that, each night, when his heavy body rested on top of Estelle, his wide, rough hand would return to the lump. I imagined his touch. I wondered if Estelle thought about why her husband's hand returned nightly to her right breast.

I felt small shocks through my stomach when I thought of them together this way.

And then Estelle began to bleed and cramp. When everything was said and done, Estelle miscarried and the doctor found the lump. Things fell from there. Soon, everyone in the building learned that the superintendent had found the lump first and not said a word. Out of guilt, or shame, he owned up to his secret.

My mother accused the superintendent of crimes against Estelle; it seemed she knew the story in ways I didn't understand.

"They got it all," the superintendent said.

"That's what the surgeons always say. They never get it all," my mother said.

The superintendent told everyone the news, and cried each time, tears of pure joy, until he was out of tears. He didn't seem to doubt the prognosis, not at all.

My mother said he killed Estelle by keeping his mouth shut. There was no point in asking my mother what she meant because she wouldn't talk to me about it. My mother was superstitious and talking about things made them happen. Secrets were big in our family. We owned a lot of books so I looked up what was going to happen to Estelle and understood my mother's fear.

They were poor. They lived in the basement apartment with all the clanging from the radiators and the boilers. Estelle wore threadbare housedresses. Her breasts were tiny, sad little things, invisible in her loose garments after years of feeding infants. I pictured the cancer they removed as a lump of coal in a wet sock. If they hadn't gotten it all, what was there left to get? The surgeon had removed the offending breast, its armpit and the muscles in her chest and back.

Estelle seemed transparent after that, like I could see through her, like she was already a goner. I had no problem creating my own horrific scenarios about Estelle's fate. I wanted to grow large beautiful breasts of my own, as quickly as possible. My mother had to wear a longline bra because her breasts were double Ds.

I spent hours in front of the bathroom mirror staring at my flat chest. I ran my hands over the rise of ribs into the shallow valleys between. I pressed and pushed my puny flesh into something resembling cleavage. I was convinced that anything I didn't recognize from the day before was cancer. Pretty soon my chest was covered in bruises the size of my fingertips, which my mother discovered. She became hysterical and hauled me off to the doctor to reassure herself there was nothing wrong with me. The doctor told me there was nothing wrong and suggested to my mother that she talk to me and explain things. My mother gave him his seven dollars and both of us left his office.

My mother did not explain anything to me that day. She did not explain anything any other day.

Six months after they took off Estelle's right breast, they took off the left, and, while they were at it, they traveled south for her uterus and ovaries. It appeared my mother was right; they never got it all. We rarely saw Estelle's gorked face around the building anymore. When we did, it was the superintendent who pushed her around in a wheelchair. She was all teeth and skull draped in tight skin. Her cancer cells were the busiest part of her, reproducing themselves exponentially faster than any other cell in her body.

Meanwhile, my breasts still swam in a double A training bra. I didn't think the bra was training my breasts to do anything, so I stuffed them with toilet paper. No one at school seemed to notice my toilet-paper enhanced breasts except Joey, Estelle's oldest son, who was one year older than me. I deliberately stuck my chest out when I saw him.

I knew Estelle's kids, but they weren't my friends. They kept to themselves, played together, helped their father around the building while Estelle dressed and fed them all. They avoided eye contact. They played hit-the-penny with a worn Spalding on the street in front of our building or roller-skated down the five block hill to the park behind it. I used the same hill, skated every day after school after homework and piano practice, that is when it wasn't raining or snowing.

I wanted to skate with Joey, race him down that hill, but didn't have the nerve to ask. My best friend was already tongue-kissing her boyfriend and I had to force myself to talk to Joey. I was skinny, with dark hair in a pixie cut. I didn't think I was pretty at all. I made friends with other kids in school – a boy with a hairlip, a girl with a club foot, a girl with Hodgkin's disease. They followed me around from class to class, walking home. I felt sorry for them. But it was Joey who held my interest.

I reasoned that Estelle's kids needed someone to play with besides each other. I was curious and scared and I felt sorry for them and I thought I would be doing a good thing, that maybe I'd be guaranteed safe passage because of doing a good thing. I finally mustered up the courage and asked Estelle's oldest boy to skate with me; we challenged each other to a race down that hill to the park. "Yeah," he said. His voice squawked unexpectedly, from soprano to tenor. "I always wanted to skate with you," he said. I smiled – at his voice and because I was a champion on that hill. I looked at him like he was a starving puppy, too happy that I'd asked him, that maybe I liked him, and like all he had were brothers and sisters and a dying mother.

So we got to skating and talking.

"Do you like Elvis?" he asked.

I was ashamed to tell him that I wasn't allowed to listen to rock n roll, only classical. My mother was a concert pianist. We went to the opera every Friday night where she made enemies, justifiably, with all the knitters who brought their yarn and needles to the performance, clacking them through every row of knit, purl, and aria. My mother embarrassed me wherever we went. I wanted to pretend I didn't know her, but obviously I was not an alone little girl. I belonged to her. Of course I listened to rock n roll when she wasn't around and I could imitate Elvis' velvet voice doing "Love Me Tender". So I sang Joey a few bars. He was cute in a blond, skinny, non-Jewish way. He looked at me, at my face, not my chest-me, and I sang the entire song, pretended to hold a microphone and swiveled my hips slowly.

He laughed and clapped.

"That was great. My dad told me your mother played the piano really good and I was supposed to respect her."

I thought about that. She was my mother and keeping the peace was high on my list of priorities, but that anyone else should have to respect her because she was a pianist confused me. I shrugged my shoulders and bent down to put on my skates.

"We should get ready," I said.

We practiced, screwing our skates into the soles of our shoes. We wore the keys around our necks, skating down that hill every day, one block at a time. Finally we moved off the sidewalk and onto the street. I could see heat sparks flying from our skates. It seemed really steep and a long way down. I crouched. So did Joey. We were bombs and the world at the bottom of the hill was our target.

The day of the race arrived. All the kids in the building turned out. And my mother was there.

"Don't get hurt." She wagged her pointer finger in my face. "You know I'm not happy about this." She never hesitated to tell me when she was unhappy with a decision of mine, and I knew she was as unhappy with my new friendship as she was about the race.

As if to disprove my mother's contention that the superintendent wanted to kill Estelle, he brought her to the event.

Joey and I started together, picking up speed, the thrill of it rushing up and through me. We both screamed and ended the race together, laughing, happy, hugging, Joey hanging on to me too tight. Since my toilet paper breasts were dissolving in my sweat, I figured I should kiss him so he wouldn't notice. I leaned my head toward his. His mouth was ready and his tongue tickled the inside of my lips. I would have stayed like that forever but the superintendent raced by, pushing Estelle in her tipped-back wheelchair. Her head was thrown back and she laughed and laughed. This was the last dance on her dance card and all I saw was love.

About Evelyn Sharenov

Ms. Sharenov is a native New Yorker and graduate of the Hunter College literature department. She was admitted to the Thomas

Hunter Scholar Program. After realizing she wanted to write, she understood her father's frequent finger-wagging statement. "You know, money doesn't grow on trees." And it takes a lot of money to support yourself as a writer. In a 180 degree turnabout, she moved to Oregon and graduated from the Oregon Health Sciences University with an advanced degree in psychiatric nursing. She never looked back at the wisdom of the degree that could go anywhere. Her writing has been published in the New York Times, the Bellevue Literary Review, Opiate. Fugue, Oregon Humanities Magazine and the Dr. TJEcklburg Review out of Johns Hopkins Univ. They invited her to read her work on their stage and she feels that was her most proud moment. She enjoys her life in the west, with the greenery, her animals, the natural beauty of the land and the waters of the Pacific Northwest. She is an active member of the NBCC and the Pacific Northwest Association of Science Writers. When she isn't writing, she is an accomplished pianist and animal activist. She admits that she's tired of city life and would enjoy having a small farm.

2

Because I Was There

CHRISTINA HOAG

Teen Sexually Assaulted at Reserve

My head cartwheels when I see the headline in the Monday edition of the Indian Valley Weekly News. It can't be. No way. It has to be something else. *Has to.*

The din in the Burger-O-Rama dulls to a seashell roar in my ears as I read on, my eyes drawn to the black type like magnets.

> *A 19-year-old woman was sexually assaulted Friday night at a popular party hangout spot at the Indian Valley Mountain Reserve, police said.*
>
> *The victim, whose identity is being withheld, was found by a park ranger in a dazed state as she wandered lost in the woods early Saturday morning. She reported that she had been sexually assaulted.*
>
> *Indian Valley police said the investigation is ongoing and no further details were available. Anyone with any information is urged to contact police.*

I feel socked in the gut. I can barely suck in any air. It's not something else. It's the same thing. And the fact is, I do have information.

Because I was there.

I look up at the sound of metal jangling. Morgan is sliding into the bench in front of me, bangles cascading on her wrists.

"What's up with you, Jade? You look like your cat died or something." She slurps her chocolate shake.

"I kind of feel sick all of a sudden."

"Cramps?"

"Nah, must be something I ate."

She glances at the newspaper lying on the table between us and stabs the story I'd just read with a forefinger. "You see that somebody got raped up at the reservation Friday night? Everybody's talking about it."

I manage a nod.

"I wonder who it was. We might even know them. Maybe Chloe knows. Looks like she wrote the story. I'll ask her."

Morgan whips out her cell phone before I have a chance to say anything. She thumbs in a message to our friend who's doing an internship as a reporter at the Weekly News this summer. The message whooshes off. Morgan puts the phone down and frowns at me.

"You really don't look so hot. You want a cup of water?"

"No. Well, maybe, yeah."

"I'll get it for you." She sidles out of the booth. Her phone beeps, startling me. An incoming text. I pick it up. My hands feel flimsy, like cheap cardboard.

No other details. Cops don't release names of rape victims. Heard it started @ carnival.

I drop the phone as if it's scorched my palm. Morgan returns with the water and spots the flashing phone. "That was fast."

I down the water as she reads the text out loud. She looks up, her eyes saucering. "The carnival! We were there Friday night. A lot of people were hanging out drinking later on. Remember? I'm really glad we left when we did."

"Yeah." A mouse could squeak louder.

This is my cue, to come out with it, the truth that I actually didn't leave the carnival when Morgan did. I went back when she went home. But I can't. It's a boulder inside me, too big for my throat, my mouth. It's stuck.

Morgan peers at me. "You're sweating and it's practically a meat locker in here. You should go home, Jadykins. Go lie down a while."

I touch my forehead. She's right. It's clammy. "Yeah, I think I will. You won't be mad?"

"Of course not. I'll stop by Sindi's. You okay to drive?"

Truthfully, I don't know. My legs feel like overcooked spaghetti, and I wonder if I can even stand up. But I have to. I yank the unspooling threads of myself together, say goodbye to Morgan and get to my car.

I drive robotically down Indian Valley Road. I don't feel like dealing with the yammering of home—my Mom, my dog, my little brother—so I pull into the park.

I stroll to the bank of the duck pond and plonk myself down, folding my legs under the embrace of my arms. Pain shoots through my knee, bruised from my hurried stumble down the stony mountain trail. It brings back Friday night in a rush.

The cloying scent of pot and beer-sweet breath. The chill rolling off the dank lake. The yell, followed by a sharp crack that made me freeze for a moment then double my pace down the slope. As I tripped down the hill, I told myself that it could be anything—a rock thrown, a branch snapped.

But in the well of my belly, I knew something wasn't right, but I chose to justify it, ignore it, forget about it, but I can't do that now. The shout ricochets around my brain: "Get off me!" The slaps echoing off the rock.

I should have gone back. I should've called the police when I got the phone signal back at the road as I waited for the Uber. I shouldn't have left her alone with that guy in the first place. But I didn't do any of that.

She must really hate me now. Still, if she hadn't started making out with that guy, I probably would've stayed. The other dude, Quint, who was obviously meant for me to pair up with, had passed out on the rock. I was cold, bored, tired so I left. Was I totally to blame? That girl wasn't really my friend anyway. I'd just met her.

My phone chirps. It's a text from Mom. "I need the car to go to my book club."

A gush of irritability swells in me as I get to my feet. Now you need the car. If you'd needed the car Friday night, then I would've driven with Morgan and I would've left the carnival when she did and this mess never would have happened. I check myself as I limp to the parking lot, my knee screaming. I'm being totally irrational. It's not my mom's fault. It's mine.

The underlying truth of the whole thing sears me as I start the car: If I tell what happened, I'll be blamed for it. People will think I'm as bad as the rapist.

I turn into my street, half expecting a police car to be in my driveway, but there's just the neighbor kid's tricycle lying on its side. I resist the urge to run it over as I pull in, and walk into the kitchen, depositing the keys on the counter. "Here you go, Mom."

"Thanks, sweetie. By the way, there was a sexual assault up at the Reserve last weekend. It was probably at that big boulder next to the lake." My heart clutches. How does she always nail this stuff? "It's a shame. It's a nice place, but it's always been a hangout for the rough crowd, even back in my day. They should just fence the whole place off. I hope you and your friends don't go there. You have to be really careful."

"We don't hang out there, Mom." That, at least, is true enough. I slink out of the kitchen under the weight of my untold lies before they crush me right there on the tile floor.

I fling myself on my bed. Caitlin, her name was Caitlin, and she had greasy hair but a smile that made her face blossom. I watched her win at the duck shooting game three times in a row at the carnival. "Hey, you're good," I said.

We started talking, then two guys came over. She introduced them to me so I figured they were her friends. The tall guy with a beard was Corky, and a shorter stockier sidekick, Quint. They were all older than me so when Keith invited us to hang out and drink some beers, and Caitlin hooked me with her eyes, I felt flattered.

There's a rap at my door. "Hey Jade, it's me."

Morgan. I unpeel myself from the bed and open up. "I just wanted to see how you were, plus I have an update." She walks in.

I figure Sindi wasn't home so lacking anything better to do, she decided to drop in on me. I flop back on the bed. "I think I'm worse, tell you the truth."

"I just got a text from Chloe. They caught the rapist."

I bolt upright. "They did?"

Morgan's busy with her phone. "There's a story on the website. Look." She hands me her phone.

> *Arrest Made in Attack on Woman*
>
> *A 21-year-old Crystal Lake man has been arrested in connection with an alleged sexual assault that occurred over the weekend at the Indian Valley Mountain Reserve.*
>
> *Keith Laird was taken into custody at his home late Sunday night and is being held for questioning in connection with the alleged attack on a 19-year-old woman, police said.*
>
> *Police said they are seeking another man in connection with the alleged assault, as well as a female witness identified only as 'Jane.'*

My stomach does that rollercoaster thing. I hope I'm not going to be sick.

"You know any Janes?" Morgan asks when I hand back her phone.

I shake my head as my heart pounds my ribs like it's going to leap out.

But I know a *Jade*.

"Me neither." She scrunches her face like she's going through the yearbook in her head.

I lie back on the bed. Should I tell her? If I do, she'll be mad at me for lying to her and pretending to leave the carnival. She'll yell at me for being so dumb to go off drinking with strangers. She'll think I'm a real asshole for leaving Caitlin, for not going back. Maybe she won't even want to be my friend anymore. And even if I swear her to secrecy, who am I kidding? She'll tell other people. It'll be all over the school in minutes.

Then I realize something. I don't have to tell anyone. No one knows who I am. They think my name is Jane. I'm safe! Wait, did I tell her anything else about me? I remember telling her my friends and I come to the carnival opening night every year, and that my friend left early and I didn't feel like going home.

I'm pretty sure I didn't tell her anything factual that could trace me, like that I'm seventeen, going to be a senior at Indian Valley High and that I work at the library, especially not that. It's a nerdy job if ever there was one. We just talked about the carnival then the guys showed up.

I instantly feel about a hundred pounds lighter. I smash a pillow over my face to stifle a bubble of laughter.

"What are you doing?"

I uncover my face to see Morgan giving me a weird look. "Nada. I'm feeling a little better."

"That's good. Well, I better get going. I have to work the early shift tomorrow."

I see her to the front door. When I return to my room, I jam my headphones on, crank up the volume and happy dance to Beyoncé until I can't catch my breath.

I wake up that night with the weight of a dumbbell pressing on my chest. My lungs scrape for air. I try to call for Mom, but my voice strangles in my throat. Somehow, she hears me and bursts into my room. Sitting by my side, she rubs my back until the attack subsides.

"It's a just a bad dream," she says. "A nightmare. It's not real."

But it is. It is realer than real.

In the morning Mom gives me a worried look as I sit at the kitchen table and grab the cornflakes box. "How are you feeling?"

"Fine," I say as I pour the cereal into the bowl. "Just a bad dream."

"I noticed an odd Uber charge on the bank statement. Twenty-two dollars from just after midnight Friday. I thought you were at the carnival with Morgan that night."

I trot out the story I've prepared, knowing she'd notice the charge. I'm supposed to use Uber only in emergencies. That night certainly qualified, though I can't tell her exactly how.

"We went to Sindi's house after the carnival in Morgan's car. When we went to go home, her car wouldn't start. I finally had to take Uber back to my car in the carnival parking lot."

"Twenty-two bucks for such a short distance?"

"It was surge pricing because it was the carnival opening night. Everybody was Ubering."

"You never told me any of that."

"I guess I forgot."

I bury my head in my cornflakes, feeling a pang of guilt over my glibness and for so easily getting away with the fib. She believes me because I always tell her the truth, almost always anyway. I just want that night to go away so I don't have to tell any more lies. Then I remember, the cops got the guy. It's over with. I can slam the door on this and forget it ever happened. I sprinkle more sugar on my cornflakes.

• • •

Morgan and I are floating on noodles in Sindi's pool two days later. The water is warm as syrup.

"So, did you see? They let that guy go, the Reserve rape guy," Sindi says from her inflatable lounger.

I perk up my head from the cradle of my arms on the noodle. "How could they let him go?"

"They had no evidence that it was rape," she says. "That's what story says."

The sun dazzles my eyes as it flashes across my mind what must've happened. There was no evidence because "Jane" was the only witness who could have said it was rape. And they never found "Jane." She never came forward.

"I still wonder who the girl was," Morgan says.

Anger pops inside me. "What does it matter who she was? It could have been you, me, any of us."

"Well, it wasn't," Morgan says.

"They shouldn't have let him go. He was guilty," I blurt. The force of my tone takes me aback.

Morgan studies me over the rim of her sunglasses. I can feel the drill of her stare, wondering why I'm so revved up about this case. I close my eyes.

"How can you be so sure? Maybe she made it up, some kind of revenge thing," Sindi says, waving off a mosquito divebombing her face. "It happens."

"Rape happens, too," Morgan says.

Then I know. I know what I should have done from the getgo because Morgan is right. Rape does happen. It can happen to anyone. It could've happened to me that night. I could've been the one who needed a witness. I could have been the one who needed to be believed.

"I am sure," I say. "Because I was there."

About Christina Hoag

Christina Hoag is the author of two novels — *Girl on the Brink,* named to Suspense Magazine's Best YA list, and *Skin of Tattoos,* Silver Falchion Award finalist. She also co-authored the nonfiction book *Peace in the Hood: Working with Gang Members to End the Violence.* A former journalist, she reported from Latin America for Time, Financial Times, New York Times and other media. Her short stories and essays have been published in numerous literary journals. She recently won honorable mentions for essay and short story in the International Human Rights Arts Festival Literary Awards 2020.

https://www.christinahoag.com

Other books/publications:

YA novels:

Girl on the Brink

Skin of Tattoos

3

Excerpt from "Sky, Full of Stars"

HAYLEY ST. JAMES

(This is an edited excerpt from a forthcoming full-length one-person play, "Sky, Full of Stars." The actress playing Sky plays every role in the play.)

SKY places her phone on a table next to a speaker, then sits down in a chair. The first verse and chorus of Coldplay's song "Life in Technicolor ii" play. She vibes to the verse, sings along with the chorus and laughs, then pauses the music to drink something from a red Solo cup she pulls out of a prop box.

SKY

"Life in Technicolor ii," from the *Prospekt's March* EP.

It's the opening instrumental track of *Viva La Vida*, extended, with lyrics. It's one of their best songs. And it immediately makes me think of my last summer before college.

• • •

The lights shift and change gel color. We're having a flashback.

It's June. I am an awkward, gangly, mess of a teenager. I haven't had my first kiss yet, but I have been to a Coldplay concert.

Because of course I have. It was my first concert, too. They gave out live CDs after the show, and I was naive and thought every concert did that.

Nope. I was just a really dumb teenager.

High school was a rollercoaster. I don't love talking about it most of the time, but the end of senior year… that was when things changed for me.

Senior year. I got a B+ in AP Psychology, got into my safety school for college and was planning to major in history or psych or something. And I had the worst crush on my chorus teacher, Mr. Benjamin. Mr. Benjamin… looked a lot like Chris Martin. Same blue eyes, same blondish hair. He sang really well.

He's a chorus teacher. Of course he sang well.

A bunch of the popular girls who looked like Taylor Swift clones and took chorus class just to get an easy passing grade teased me mercilessly for thinking Mr. Benjamin looked like Chris Martin. I got a solo in our end of the year concert. It was something haunting—probably by Eric Whitacre, since it wasn't in Latin or Italian as so many of our other usual chorus songs were—and the blonde bitches said the only reason I got the solo was because I tried to be Mr. Benjamin's teacher's pet.

• • •

I wasn't trying to be—I just never checked my texts during chorus. I was one of those students whose best friends were mostly their teachers, not other students. I thought if you became friends with your teachers that'd help you get into college.

Senior year I was still struggling with my sexuality—as I said, never been kissed at this point—and, looking back now, I feel so bad I can't just time travel back in a TARDIS and go "hey! Sky! Stop crushing on your chorus teacher! You like girls! The only men you will ever truly like are the guys from Coldplay!", an then pop back to now and see if anything changed.

Maybe that's cause of some sorta butterfly effect thing and I won't end up with any of the same stories. But it's Coldplay. Butterflies are sort of their thing. In that case, maybe the butterfly effect wouldn't happen after all.

Okay. So. My end of high school senior year party. It's being hosted by one of the popular girls, my frequent classmate Kitty Harviton. She invited me because —

KITTY

My mom insisted I invite everyone in the graduating class, to be "inclusive."

SKY

Of course, when I get to the party, the parents are conveniently out of town and every kid at the party is drinking. Everything feels like a stereotypical teen movie. I have never had liquor before that night, and it's the end of senior year, OF COURSE I want to have drinks, I want to be cool and accepted and fun before I head off to college and never see any of these people who made fun of me behind their backs ever again! So I get a red Solo cup of rum and Coke from the kitchen island, take a sip — it's like regular Coke but with a vanilla-y throat burn at the end of it, not bad — and proceed to wander around the party, mostly people watching and kind of hoping no one actually notices me.

Deep down, I kind of wanted to be noticed, for once.

SKY takes another sip from her Solo cup.

I'm wearing a tank top and short shorts. I'm extremely self conscious about my body—my boobs aren't small enough and my legs are too long for my otherwise short body. I hate exposing this much skin, mostly because I got nightmares after reading so many depressing young adult books about girls being hit on or taken advantage of by boys at parties.

So I take another sip of rum and Coke, put one of my arms around my chest, and keep watching kids at the party. One of the Taylor Swift clones is fighting with her lacrosse team boyfriend while "Get Lucky" by Daft Punk blasts on the sound system. Another decently popular girl, from my AP Psych class, is making out with my lab partner from my junior year biology class.

I silently wish I was invited to the drama kids' party instead. I liked them, even if they didn't talk to me as much, plus it'd be a lot less...

heterosexual. Or loud.

Maybe the drama kids would actually play music I liked. Daft Punk isn't bad. It just isn't Coldplay.

I go to the bathroom, lock myself in, and I put my iPod on and turn on my playlist.

First song, "Life in Technicolor ii." I let the Brian Eno-produced sound wash over me. It calms me down, a bit.

SKY plays the second verse of "Life in Technicolor ii" but hits pause before the chorus.

I finish my entire rum and Coke in one massive, painful gulp, toss the cup in the bathroom trash can, and exit the bathroom. I keep my earbuds in and let my music play.

SKY throws the empty Solo cup into the prop box and gets up out of the chair.

I go out to the backyard, where some of the football boys have set up a fire pit and are drinking from a keg someone snuck in.

Between the keg and the rum and Cokes I wonder where all these underage kids got all the liquor from.

Fake IDs?

Maybe.

I shrug it off. I suppose all teen parties are like this.

And then, I see her. Standing by some trees on the other side of the yard, drinking out of a Solo cup and not talking to anyone in particular. Just swaying, vibing with the music, her eyes closed.

Kris Harviton.

Kris is Kitty Harviton's sister. Kris looks nothing like Kitty — where Kitty is blonde and immaculate and reeks of artificial teenage femininity, Kris is a lot softer, and more human looking. Kitty's hot, sure, but Kris is CUTE. Even now I can't believe they're sisters. Fraternal twins.

She's wearing a crop top and high waisted jeans. She has a flannel tied around her waist.

I can see her stomach. It's soft and round and pokes out a bit. It looks like mine.

And softly lit by the flames of the fire pit, she looks… gorgeous.

Suddenly, everything makes sense.

The second chorus of "Life in Technicolor ii" blares. SKY takes in the music. She's smitten all over again. She lets the song play to the end, then pauses it when the song finishes.

• • •

The thing is, Kris and I were friends, once. In elementary school. She was maybe the closest thing I had to a best friend. We had playdates and I invited her to all my birthday parties and vice versa until I was like, eleven. I was never super close with Kitty, but she came to the parties too, because her mom and my mom insisted.

Kris was shy, but super gifted. I thought I was pretty smart, I read a lot for a kid my age. But Kris… she was a genius. Put her hand up to answer the teachers' questions before anyone else. Even me. She read books grade levels above our own. She didn't talk in class otherwise. And I admired that about her. I admired her filter.

Once we both got to middle school, Kris changed schools. She went to one of those year-round STEM-centric boarding schools. So Kitty became the Harviton sister in all my classes, and I didn't see Kris for years. She sent me a few emails early on, but stopped returning my replies after a while. I figured our friendship was on hold. I moved on. At least, I thought I did.

With Kris away at another school, Kitty got popular at ours.

I think — no, I *know* — Kitty got popular because she got boobs before any other girl in our grade.

I absolutely noticed. Both her getting popular and her getting boobs.

That may have been the first time I realized I wasn't straight. But I was twelve. I didn't know anything. I guess now I'd call it a crush? But I shrugged that off as a twelve year old. I just thought to myself, "oh. Kitty got boobs. *Nice.*" And that was that.

• • •

SKY thinks about boobs for a second. SKY smiles. Then she snaps back to the story at hand.

Senior year party. Right.

Kris, standing in the yard, gently lit by the flames. Surrounded by teenage boys doing keg stands.

This is the first time I've seen Kris since she left for boarding school.

The last time I saw her she was small and wore big glasses that took up almost two thirds of her head that made her look like a cartoon character.

Seven years later, she's not wearing glasses anymore and I can see her perfect, freckled skin lit by the firelight.

She opens her eyes and notices me across the yard.

Kris smiles and waves at me.

I feel like my stomach is about to implode on itself. Really regretting drinking my entire rum and Coke in the bathroom.

But then I realize it's not the drink making me feel weird.

It's the butterflies in my stomach.

Like the confetti at the Coldplay concert.

I take my earbuds out and run over to Kris's side of the yard.

Before I can even say anything to her, Kris hugs me so hard I can barely breathe. She hugs me for what seems like an hour to my drunk brain but, in actuality, it was probably a few seconds, then breaks, breathlessly.

KRIS

Oh my god. Sky. How many years has it been? I'm so glad you're here —

SKY (to audience)

She talks rapid-fire, like a machine gun. She was never this chatty when we were younger.

(to KRIS)

Kris! It's been forever, I'm glad you're here too —

KRIS

I can't believe Kitty invited you —

SKY

I can't believe you're here, I've missed you so much —

• • •

KRIS

I can't believe you're here, I've missed YOU so much —

SKY

Seven years, huh? Wild.

KRIS

Wild.

SKY

(to audience)

Kris searches my face. She takes in seven years of acne scarring and over-plucked eyebrows.

Then, she says, out of nowhere —

KRIS

Party's kind of boring, want to hang in my room?

SKY

(to audience)

And my heart just. Starts beating so fast.

(to KRIS)

Yeah. Sure. Totally. Keg stands terrify me.

KRIS

Same.

SKY

(to audience)

And, with that, Kris takes my hand, holding her cup in the other.

My heart beats extremely fast.

Girl holding my hand. Oh gosh, oh gosh, oh gosh.

She leads me past the keg stand boys, back into the house, past other partygoers, and up the stairs to the hallway where her bedroom is.

Kitty's door across from Kris's is shut, but there's ambient light coming from under the door frame.

I think briefly about the fact that I haven't seen Kitty once this evening. I bet she looks hot.

The thought passes.

The music from downstairs is still quite loud even from the second floor.

We're in Kris's room. I haven't been in here since elementary school.

She still has the same pale peach wallpaper and popcorn ceiling, and a twin bed covered in stuffed animals.

We sit on the shaggy grey rug on the floor.

SKY sits back down in the chair.

(to KRIS)

Your room's the same.

KRIS

Well, when you go to a year-round boarding school and a sleep-away camp during the summer... not much room for change.

SKY

(to audience)

The energy shifts as she says that. The years of not interacting with her at all makes what was so soft and warm outside seem colder.

(to KRIS)

All this time and you never thought to text me?

KRIS

I didn't get a cellphone until I started upper school.

• • •

SKY

I would have always been down to text. I missed you SO much, Kris. You have zero idea how hard it was to make friends in middle school and high school.

KRIS

I feel so awful about it. I really do.

I should have reached out to ask for your number. But I didn't. Don't know why I didn't ask my sister or something. Schoolwork was everything to me while I was there. I barely used my phone for anything except listening to music and calling my family.

I only *just* got Facebook because I didn't want colleges to stalk me during the application process.

I did send you a few emails at the beginning, at least.

SKY

Fair enough. I still haven't deleted any of them.

(to audience)

I watch as Kris downs her entire rest of her rum and Coke in an instant and flings her cup across the room into a waste basket by the door.

My heart is still beating so fast from her holding my hand outside, I just have to impulsively change the topic at hand.

• • •

(to KRIS)

Your music taste's still the same?

KRIS

You know it. Pretty much just… Coldplay.

SKY

(to audience)

When we were kids, like elementary school age, Kris and I listened to a lot of Coldplay. We heard "Clocks" on the sound system at a McDonald's once and never looked back. No one else our age really listened to them, but we didn't care. If the adult world loved them as much as us, we felt cool. Loving this band at such a young age was our little secret.

Back to the party.

Kris takes her phone out of her jeans pocket and pulls a Bluetooth speaker, like one you'd use in the shower, out of her Jansport backpack flung into the center of an indigo blue beanbag chair in the corner. She scootches closer to me. I can smell the rum and Coke on her breath, it's a sweet and warm, almost cinnamon scent. Like Christmas in June.

KRIS

What era was it the last time I saw you?

• • •

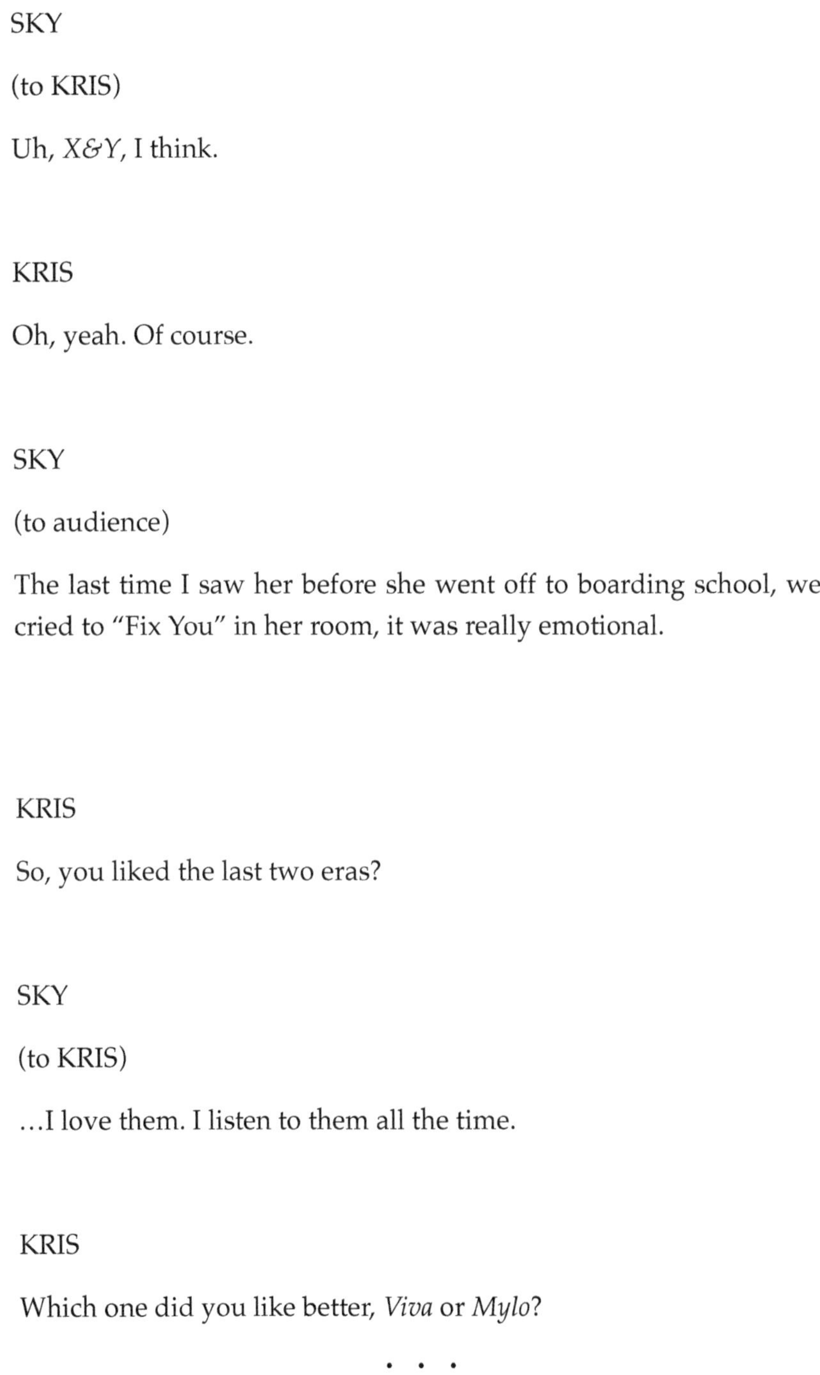

SKY

(to KRIS)

Uh, *X&Y*, I think.

KRIS

Oh, yeah. Of course.

SKY

(to audience)

The last time I saw her before she went off to boarding school, we cried to "Fix You" in her room, it was really emotional.

KRIS

So, you liked the last two eras?

SKY

(to KRIS)

...I love them. I listen to them all the time.

KRIS

Which one did you like better, *Viva* or *Mylo*?

• • •

SKY

Both. I like both pretty much equally. If Brian Eno doesn't come back for LP6 I think I might riot. Brian has really reshaped how the band sounds. They sound better than they ever have.

KRIS

Oh for sure. I think I liked *Mylo* a bit more, it's so different from how any of the previous eras sound—so bright and whimsical and interesting.

SKY

Viva is just... phenomenal, though, don't you agree? Those Grammys speak for themselves.

KRIS

Oh, absolutely.

SKY

When they were nominated for the Best Rock Album Grammy one of the metalhead boys in my 8th grade science class picked on me for weeks because he was *so* confident Metallica was going to win.

KRIS

And then Coldplay won, I remember! I bet that boy had no idea what hit him.

• • •

SKY

I gloated so much the Monday after. The band doesn't even know I exist but I talk about them like they're my four secret second dads, or something.

KRIS

Did you listen to the *Prospekt's March* EP too?

SKY

Funny enough, I was listening to it again before you saw me on the other side of the yard.

KRIS

What song?

SKY

"Life in Technicolor ii" —

KRIS

That's my FAVORITE off the EP!

SKY

Me too!

. . .

KRIS

Damn, I wanna listen to it right now!

SKY

(to the audience)

Kris takes my phone out of my hand and connects the speaker to my phone. "Life in Technicolor ii" resumes playing from the beginning. We let the music wash over us.

I look at her.

She looks at me.

There's something about this song that changes the energy in the room again. She takes my hand again as the song plays, and doesn't let go.

The rest of "Life in Technicolor ii" plays.

(to KRIS)

When I saw them live a few summers ago, they gave out free live CDs.

KRIS

YOU GOT A PHYSICAL COPY OF *LEFTRIGHTLEFTRIGHTLEFT*? This whole time I've had to deal with my audio rip of it from the official website that they took down after, like, a month.

SKY

I have an extra copy… if you want it. I can bring it over some time.

KRIS

Yeah. I'd love that. As long as you bring it over before we both head off to college.

SKY

Sure. Of course. And you'll be here all summer?

KRIS

Yeah. Aged out of sleep-away camp, so I have my first summer back home with my best friend in 7 years.

SKY

Awesome. We can make up for lost time.

KRIS

Yeah… lost time.

• • •

The final instrumental bridge of the song before the final chorus approaches.

SKY

(to audience)

And then, out of nowhere... she awkwardly presses her lips to mine.

My mind is on fire.

I'm having my first kiss.

And it's my best friend I haven't seen in years.

Who is a girl and not someone who looks like Chris Martin.

I have no idea what to do so I start moving my lips around hers. I do that for what feels like a while. We both kind of open our mouths a little and we have no idea what our teeth or tongues are doing but we break before it gets too sloppy.

(to KRIS)

...that was my first kiss.

KRIS

I was your first? Aw.

SKY

You've kissed other people?

• • •

KRIS

At sleep-away camp. Just once. With a boy. Truth or dare at the campfire. Not particularly good.

SKY

I'm sorry.

KRIS

It's okay.

...was that kiss okay?

SKY

Yeah. It was nice.

(to audience)

We sit there for a few seconds as the second track from the *Prospekt's March* EP, the piano instrumental "Postcards from Far Away," begins to play. We fumble into a few more shorter kisses, minus all the tongue and teeth business. It all only lasts as long as the song—forty-eight seconds, and when we break and the song ends Kris gets up from the rug and stretches. Her stomach rises, her crop top shifts up a little and... I look down at the rug and blush profusely before I can see anything else.

• • •

KRIS

Wanna head back downstairs and see if the other kids have done anything stupid?

SKY

(to KRIS)

Yeah. Sure.

(to audience)

I slip my phone in my pocket, get up, and take Kris's hand. We head out her door and are about to close it and head down the steps back to the party when —

KITTY

Kris? What were you doing in your room with Sky Full Of Stars? The party's downstairs.

SKY

Kitty and Evan McBain, a boy from the wrestling team I've only ever seen in passing in the hallway, have exited Kitty's bedroom. Evan looks kind of exhausted and dead-eyed. Kitty's hair is in a messy ponytail and her senior class t-shirt is haphazardly clinging to her.

Her boobs look… really nice.

But I shrug the thought off.

I just kissed her sister.

Can't think about both. That'd be weird.

Also, Sky Full Of Stars was what the popular girls called me as some sort of nickname. Appropriate in hindsight, considering it ended up being the name of a Coldplay single a year later.

(to KITTY)

Hey, Kitty. Kris just wanted to show me —

KRIS

I wanted to show Sky a video I saw on Youtube I've been meaning to show her for a few years now! What were you and Evan doing?

KITTY

Two player beer pong?

KRIS

On your bed? Riiiiiight. Beer pong. That's what they call it.

KITTY

Do *not* tell Mom. God, it's so WEIRD having you back here. Hope you're having fun, Sky.

• • •

SKY

(to audience)

We watch as Kitty and Evan head down the stairs. Then, we look at each other as they stumble back to the party and out of sight.

(to KRIS)

Do you actually have a video on Youtube you wanted to show me?

KRIS

Yeah, but you've probably already seen it.

SKY

Try me.

KRIS

The music video —

SKY

For "Life in Technicolor ii"? Also my favorite. What I'd give to have those puppets crash my birthday party.

• • •

KRIS

God, same. Screw the party. Wanna rewatch it?

SKY

(to audience)

And the rest of that night was spent watching music videos and stealing kisses and catching up on lost time until I had to go home.

About Hayley St. James

Hayley St. James (they/them) is a Boston-born, usually-New York-based playwright and performer, and a graduate of Marymount Manhattan College's class of 2020. A non-binary lesbian on the autism spectrum, they are deeply passionate about seeing themselves and their communities represented truthfully in all media, theatre first and foremost. In their theatrical work, they strive to marry authentic representation with hyper-theatrical, surreal, meta, and occasionally horny twists. They also have a thing for imaginary friends, ghosts, aliens, and well-handled pop culture references. Their plays include *What A Piece of Work is Ham* (a stoner comedy prequel to William Shakespeare's Hamlet;) *Too Hard A Knot* (a twenty-minute Bard-inspired dark comedy about the choices we make in this world;) *For Leonora, or, Companions* (a tender, puppet-driven exploration of life on the autism and LGBTQ spectrum;) and *A Godawful Small Affair* (a sad, hopeful, and sexually frank quarantine play guest starring the ghost of David Bowie.)

twitter.com/@hayleystjames

PART II

What Lies Beyond - Sci-Fi Short Stories

Journey through space and time as you read selections from ***What Lies Beyond—Sci-Fi Short Stories***. In this collection of science fiction stories, you will be confronted with aliens, robots, clones, and… cats? When it comes to the ever-expanding universe and the bounds of technology, anything is possible!

1

Generalist

STEPHEN OLIVER

Mick King wandered down the corridor to the Induction Room.

It had been a long haul on his previous shift, so he was looking forward to something a bit simpler this time. He didn't hold out much hope for it, however. He was one of the best Generalists in the world, which meant that he was expected to take on the most difficult cases.

In today's world, there were so few real experts anymore who could handle even a small part of the multiple special disciplines at the same time, which was why the government made use of people like Mick.

The Generalists were people who could work in many areas at the same time, but not because they had studied them for years.

Instead, they had a condition where they were unable to retain information beyond a certain level of complexity in any one subject. Their neurological peculiarities did, however, allow them to remember vast amounts of apparently unrelated data for shorter periods of time, and to make connections between them that individual experts in those areas could not. Depending on their level of ability, this could be anywhere from six to twenty-four hours, or so.

Mick was one of the 'Day Minds', able to retain the information longer than most. That was why he got the most difficult jobs, despite functionally being an idiot.

Douglas McBrian greeted him as he entered the room.

"Hey, Big Brain, we've got a special for you today."

Mick groaned. Another long shift in the making, it appeared.

Douglas took his glasses off and gave them a quick polish, a nervous habit that Mick had observed whenever the man was under stress.

"Let's get you ready, shall we?" Douglas continued.

Mick nodded, stripped down to his singlet and shorts, then sat down in the chair under the massive machine with the wired helmet at the bottom.

Blood lines and feeding tubes connected to the permanent cannulas in his arms, legs and chest, and the catheter automatically found its way in.

Douglas rubbed an antiseptic depilatory gel over the stubble on Mick's head, removing all the hair, and sterilising the contact points dotting his skull at the same time.

A quick wipe from a dry cloth and Mick was ready for Induction.

The helmet dropped down and surrounded his entire head.

He felt the connections slip into their respective holes in his skull, clicking as they fully engaged.

A shiver passed through him. It always did when he was connected to the Inducer. He could never be sure if it was fear or excitement.

"Ready, Mick?" Douglas asked, his voice passing directly into Mick's brain through the helmet.

"As I'll ever be," Mick replied the same way, bypassing his vocal cords.

He sensed rather than heard Douglas type in the activation code.

The chair began to move backward, slowly turning into a recliner-like bed to support his body without strain.

Information poured into his brain, overwhelming all his senses, so that he existed only in a swirl of facts and data, all demanding entry into his mind.

Training took over and he opened the 'doors' to let them in.

For an unknown period, he was bombarded with everything.

He became aware of his surroundings as the front of the helmet lifted away and information screens lowered in front of his face.

As always, it all looked different, because the information was distorting his perceptions in ways he had never felt before.

He knew everything, again, even if only for a short time.

It looked like today's first problem had to do with social dynamics and the predictability of the mass interactions of human beings in political cycles, with a special emphasis on voting trends.

Even as he considered all the data flowing through his brain, as he processed the information, he noticed a certain similarity in the way everything fluxed and shifted from day to day during an election cycle. There was a strong resemblance to the formation of mega-waves; waves over a hundred feet high that appeared spontaneously out of nowhere in the middle of oceans. A quick data request confirmed that a prediction was theoretically possible using the Schrödinger Wave Equation, something used in Quantum Theory to calculate the probabilities of electron motion. He applied it to older information and saw that future predictions compared with the newer data were within acceptable sigma limits.

Once he had passed this on to the computers, he felt the problem clearing from his mind, even though all the knowledge remained.

After a minute, a new problem appeared in his consciousness: how to increase the sensitivity of orbital gravitational telescopes, so that they could detect unaccompanied neutron stars, blazars and black holes out beyond the present limit of half a billion light years. He shuffled through his brain and found an answer within three minutes.

His thoughts cleared again, and another problem was presented. Then another. And another…

He realised that his shift must be coming to an end when he felt knowledge slipping away from him. He could no longer access it as quickly or accurately.

He willed himself to press the 'Stop' button under his left thumb.

As always, his body felt very slow and sluggish in comparison to the speed at which he could think while in the *induced* state.

The chair moved back to a more upright position, and the helmet disengaged its connections from his skull and lifted itself away from him.

Douglas stepped in front of him and started to disconnect the tubes from Mick's body. It was obviously the next day because his shirt was green, whereas it had been yellow the day before.

"A good session," he commented as he glanced at the display. "Twenty-five and a half hours. You're getting better at this."

"Huh?" Mick replied. As the knowledge fled his brain, he felt slow and stupid, back to his usual subnormal intelligence.

"You did good, Mick," Douglas said. He knew that Mick was already well into *Defluxing Mode* by now and would be unable to respond normally for a while. "Why don't you take the evening off?"

Mick paused as he was dressing himself.

"You wanna come have a drink with me?"

Douglas looked up from the monitor screens and across at Mick.

"Why not?" he replied with a smile. "I've got nothing else to do."

The report he wiped off the screen showed that Mick had been performing at optimum again. He had no idea how much longer the man would last at this intensity and he felt sad. The day would come when Mick's nervous system would not be able to process data the way the bosses wanted. On that day, Mick would be 'retired' to a facility for the feeble-minded, to while away his days doing simple things until he died.

Then, his brain would be autopsied to determine what was so special about it. The bosses wanted to know how they could create more Generalists, instead of having to wait until they found them by accident.

Douglas had heard rumours, however, that ex-Generalists did not survive their 'retirement' for very long…

Douglas smiled at Mick as they left the lab and walked around the corner to the bar. It was a special place reserved for Generalists and their support staff. All drinks for the Generalists were alcohol free, although they didn't taste like it, to keep the possibilities of brain damage to a minimum.

Mick ordered two beers as they walked over to the table in their usual alcove. He didn't notice the minor differences between his and Douglas's glasses as he took a long swallow.

"Ah, that's good," he said as he wiped the foam off his upper lip. "I need a brewski or two to unwind."

"You've got it easy," Douglas smiled in return. "You get to lie around all day, while I'm running around making sure you're okay."

"Yeah. You're so good to me. Why do you do it?"

That was an awkward question for Douglas, who was highly paid to keep Mick happy and productive. He took his spectacles off and began polishing them.

"I like you," he replied after the merest hesitation. "You've got an important job to do and I'm proud to be allowed to help you to do it." That much was the truth. He just hoped that Mick would never find out that he was his minder, tasked with keeping him going for as long as possible before his brain burned out.

"Hey, are you okay?" he asked Mick.

Mick was staring at a man who was glaring at him.

The man stood up and strode over to their table to lean menacingly over Mick.

"What you lookin' at, Mac," he growled.

Mick cowered beneath that angry gaze.

"Nothing," he replied.

"Well, from where I'm sittin', it looked like you was oglin' my girl."

"I wasn't," Mick began, then subsided as the man leant even closer to him.

"Excuse me," Douglas said as he stood up.

The man rounded on him.

"Stay out of this, Four Eyes," he shouted. "It ain't your business."

He put a large hand in the middle of Douglas's chest and pushed hard, forcing him to sit down again. He turned back to Mick, knocked the beer glass out of his hand, and cocked his fist.

"You're gonna get it now, and good," he shouted.

In the meantime, Douglas tapped twice on the face of his watch, sending an emergency signal out to Security.

Two seconds later, there was a strange *whoosh* combined with a weird reverse *thud*, and two heavily-armed and -armoured private policemen stood in the room, one on either side of the man.

He looked from one to the other, then lowered his fist.

The two policemen grasped his arms.

"Hey fellas," he began, "it didn't mean nothin'. I was only gonna rearrange his face a bit."

"Assault, or threatened assault, of a Generalist is a Class One offence," the electronically modified voice of one of the cops replied, "punishable by no less than five and no more than fifteen years in prison. You will come with us."

"Hey, I didn't know he was a freakin' Generalist, did I?" the man shouted.

"This is a bar for Generalists and their personnel only," the other policeman's identical voice said. "You will tell us how you were able to gain illegal access. Come with us."

The *whoosh* and *thud* repeated themselves as the policemen teleported themselves and the man back to the police station.

"You okay?" Douglas asked Mick.

Mick shook his head to clear it.

"I guess so," he replied. "Why was that guy so mad at me?"

Douglas shrugged.

"Maybe he wanted to be a Generalist and couldn't cut the mustard. Who knows?" He picked up his beer glass and Mick's spilt one. "Ready for another beer?"

"Sure am," Mick replied. "Any chance of some pretzels and maybe beer nuts to go with it?"

"I'll see what I can do," Douglas replied with a smile.

He could see that Mick was already getting over the shock.

It would never do for some stranger to hit Mick. After all, nobody knew what exactly it was that made a Generalist the man or woman they were. The bosses were constantly worried that any kind of brain damage might lose them one of their greatest assets. Especially one as good as Mick.

In the meantime, Mick was congratulating himself on being chosen for his career. He was one in millions. Maybe even billions.

He proved that the old adage was no longer true: 'A jack of all trades is a master of none.'

Everyday, with modern technological help, he was the master of them all!

About Stephen Oliver

Stephen's father was in the Royal Air Force during all of his childhood and youth, moving every couple of years or so, so he was always the new kid in class at school. Later, when he established himself as a software engineer, he was most often the outsider because he was the foreigner (working in Switzerland as a Brit) or the freelance consultant called in to solve a problem or three.

He spent the majority of his career as a software engineer, where he wrote specifications, programs, and handbooks. When the financial problems of the early 2010s forced him to close down his software company in 2012, he moved back from Switzerland to the UK to look after his aging parents, who were also moving back, as he had been their de facto carer for some years.

He first became aware of science fiction over fifty years ago, turning into an instant fan and remaining one ever since. A few years later, he increased his range to include fantasy and horror, plus an interest in integrative psychology and the paranormal.

Since restarting his career as a software engineer in the UK proved difficult, due to his age (mid-fifties at the time), he decided to put his love of science fiction and fantasy, as well as his ability to write clear prose, to good use and began writing fiction. He has since completed six books, revised and edited them (four anthologies forming a single series, plus two versions of a science fiction novel). He is also working on another two novels, a further three anthologies, and a second self-help book (the first, he self-published in 2013).

His favourite genres include self-help, science fiction, space opera, fantasy, urban fantasy, magical realism, horror, fairy tales, fairy stories, noir, detective fiction, humour, YA, children's stories (often more than one in any particular story!). Other works are presently in the planning stage. Over the last 8 years, he has written over 1,000,000 words.

Also by Stephen Oliver

Unleash Your Dreams

Contributor on:

The Midas Touch

Where the Wild Winds Blow

A Following Wind.

Contact Stephen Oliver

www.stephenoliver-author.com

https://www.facebook.com/stephen.oliver.940/

Smashwords: https://www.smashwords.com/books/view/682994

2

Preacher

LISA DIAZ MEYER

The preacher was profoundly different from us. He claimed he was a man from so far away that he could not point to his planet or constellation in our sky. He could have shown us if only his dashboard had not been wrecked in the crash, he said. The preacher was hurt and hungry, running low on his supplies. We tried to help, my brothers and I. We provided him with friendship, company, and questions. Like, "why was he here" and "how did he become a preacher"?

"A preacher is born a preacher," he told us. He was here to spread the word of an ancient, powerful God, one who was all goodness and kindness but needed prayers and devotion. He taught us all about his God, whom he rejoiced, who was our God as well.

"Why did your God make you crash here then?" asked Younger.

"Yes, and on a planet that hasn't any food for you?" asked Elder.

The preacher laughed at his poor luck, looking down at his bandaged knee and torn-up uniform. "It's not always in God's hands what happens, it's how you handle it."

"Ah, like a test," the three of us agreed.

The preacher could be very smart. He leaned on his staff the one Elder carved for him and stared into the darkness of our sky.

Nothing grew here, not for twenty-seven cycles, but, when our sun reaches this side of the planet, there will be lush plants and gardens so high, so green that the terrain we were standing on now would not even be recognizable. In the meantime, we lived by the brilliance of the moonlight. Our huge star reflected enough of it to appear as if daylight were provided. In less mountainous areas, we could see our closest neighbors in the black sky.

The preacher said our view was magnificent. We thanked God for it and prayed with him. He was a wonderful teacher. He spoke in quotes from the Holy Book and read the stories to us. My brothers and I were fascinated by its words and wisdom—and by the preacher himself.

The preacher required much sleep. He would amble to his destroyed cockpit and take his rest there while we went off to our nearby cavernous residence.

As time went on, his light brown hair and beard grew and grew. He always spoke so wisely and clearly, and with passion for God, while leaning on the twisted walking stick. As more time passed, the preacher grew haggard and thin. We feared for his existence and that his journey among the planets was over. There would be no others to spread the good word throughout the vast universe.

He enjoyed our company, we were told, and our eagerness to learn and follow although we were such an inferior race. We looked nothing like the preacher. He was handsome with light eyes, flowing hair, straight teeth, and a trusting smile. His arms and legs were hairy while ours were pale and slippery. Our neck and head shapes were similar but not our faces.

Compared to this man of the word, my two brothers and I looked buffoonish. Was it wrong to say we were dumb and also dumber looking? Should we not have admired our own race instead of this dazzling preacher with smallish eyes and nose and charming creases around his eyes when he smiled? Was it wrong to say he objectified beauty and I wished we looked more like him?

He joked and said we looked like "fish out of water," whatever that meant, but not a fish he'd ever seen, and he had seen many worlds and many races. The preacher said that made us unique.

His knee was healing with the patience of time—unlike his vehicle, which he attempted to fix every now and again, but it always ended in failure. The preacher was trapped with us and therefore doomed. We could not help him. We could not fix his ship. Our food was inedible to him. Our intermittent diet consisted of mainly a few minerals and rocks. Such a thing would kill him. At least he had taught us well, his verses of God. His God and our God.

One night he crawled unhappily into his ship's cockpit where he always slept, and we three brothers went to our cavern, our home, our hole in the red mountains.

When morning came, there was no sign of Younger. We called to him in our native way. He never answered. Strange, since we had always stayed within earshot. We tried again, Elder calling in a sharper, more commanding tone. Mine was more nasal, more worried and desperate. Younger was, of course, free to walk about our lands. Being the younger, he had more energy and a need to explore. But to not answer Elder's pitch? It was unlike him to ignore us both.

So the two of us set out that morning in search of Younger, mostly to berate him for not telling us where he'd gone off to. It took some time, but we finally stumbled onto the preacher's crash site.

He hopped down on his good leg. "What are you two honking about so early in the day?"

Elder looked at me, his eye squinting to show he disapproved of our calls being joked about as "honking." But that was what it was.

Just as I was to ask if the preacher had seen Younger, my eye caught his campsite not far beyond. It was usual that he would be heating a hot beverage he called coffee or a small bite to eat since he hadn't much left. But this morning there was much more smoke than usual, and the smell made me gag.

"Where is Younger?" Elder asked with heavy suspicion. I didn't understand at the moment that, as far as races go, ours were meant for happiness and not intelligence.

The preacher didn't answer, but we followed him as he limped to the campfire. I don't know how he stood the smell. Elder and I looked at what was cooking. It was as if my mind had gone mad. My innards turned. Younger was attached to the preacher's fire spit, long dead, burned, and partially eaten.

Elder and I reached for each other's slippery hands. The pain, shock, and disbelief were wholly unbearable. I hoped I might faint and awaken to find this horrible scene had been erased from my sight.

"Like I've said," the preacher announced, "God provides when you're in need."

How could he do this? The preacher had been our friend and teacher. Elder and I were speechless.

"And I am in need. I am desperate for food, my trusting, foolish friends."

I began to wail as our kind would in grief. Elder said nothing. He let me grieve. He let me feel the betrayal by this new friend. The loss of my brother, the loss of what I thought to be a great friendship, the loss of my trusting nature—I could not understand it. Without my brother or my kindness, I would never be myself again. I was lost. I loved my brother, and in different ways we both were gone.

Finally Elder dragged me away. My eyes burned from the smoke of my brother's burning corpse. At the red caverns, Elder turned to me and said, "Cry all you want, brother. That *man* was not a preacher. He is a stranger from a strange world with a God we do not need."

He was right. Elder was always the smartest of the three of us; I, the trusting one; and Younger, the kindest. "We cannot blame ourselves for his lies."

"What will we do without our brother?" I whined.

In the morning I rose with Elder, and we made for the preacher's camp. Younger still hung from the spit, but there was less of him now. I tore my sight from my brother's ravaged carcass to Elder who had quietly taken the preacher's unattended staff in hand, the very one he'd made Preacher when he'd first arrived, an aid to help him walk on his wounded leg.

Preacher lay on the ground, asleep on his stomach, facing the opposite direction. Somehow, on silent feet, Elder got close enough and slammed the head of the staff across the preacher's neck.

We scrambled around to see his face. His eyes were open, and greenish spittle and vomit hung from his twitching lips. It was the same greenish color of our skin. His two light eyes found us and in them there was surprise, fear, and panic.

"Poison," he whispered. "You are poisonous."

Elder nodded. "Your death will be slow, and while we wait, we will eat you piece by piece because to us *man* is not poisonous. You are not the first to have landed here. We too have hungered for a very long time. And so you are correct, Preacher, your God does provide."

About Lisa Diaz Meyer

Dark fiction author and poet, Lisa Diaz Meyer uses controversial topics and awarenesses in her collection of award-winning speculative fiction. Other than reading and writing she loves the theater, photography, history, museums, science fiction and horror. Born and raised in the East New York section of Brooklyn, Lisa now hails from Long Island's south shore.

Also by Lisa Diaz Meyer

ALL ROADS HOME: A Collection of Short Stories

ALL ROADS DESTINED: A Collection of Dark Fiction and Poems

ALL ROADS SHATTERED: A Collection of Dark Fiction Short Stories and Poems

Contact Lisa Diaz Meyer

Website - lisadiazmeyer.com

www.facebook.com/LDMeyerAuthorALLROADS

instagram.com/lisadiazmeyer

@LisaDMeyer

www.linkedin.com/mwlite/in/lisa-diaz-meyer-b16a81b6

3

The Felinedae Mission

DEBBIE DE LOUISE

New York City, 2030

Jezebel warned me. She didn't speak, but she communicated with me in her telepathic way. All cats are telepaths, but only certain people can interpret their messages. I, Lily Palmer, librarian, cat mystery author, and cat club president, am one of them. Jezebel informed me that something bad was coming. It was noon on a Sunday in late winter. Still in my cat pajamas, laying in bed with my laptop, I had just finished writing a *Booklist* review and was outlining a new cozy mystery in which I hoped to feature my three cats. As I was typing, Jezzy jumped on the bed causing a series of jumbled letters and exclamation marks to appear on my screen. I was about to knock her down when she turned and faced me, her green eyes aglow with urgency. With a silent meow she flashed me the message – *"Danger is coming."* The message was either that, or she wanted to be fed. Unfortunately, it turned out to be the former.

I slipped into my fuzzy Persian slippers and went into the kitchen of my small apartment. I was lucky to have grabbed this place so close to where I worked at the New York Public Library after my sister, Laura, married and moved to Long Island, leaving me with a rent-controlled lease. It was even luckier that the landlord liked cats and turned a blind eye to the fact that I had two more than were normally allowed in apartments.

Joey and Jake came to me as soon as I entered the kitchen. Joey, my five-year-old black cat, was first to eat as I poured kibble and refreshed the water bowls. Jake, my ten-year-old mackerel tabby, waited patiently while Joey finished breakfast. Jezebel, Joey's muted calico sister, having followed me from the bedroom, wound around my ankles, rubbing her cheek against my lower leg. After the cats had all finished their morning routines, I scooped the litter box that I kept in the bathroom. Although my fellow cat club members would be upset with me if they knew that I didn't have a litter box for each cat, I made sure to keep their single one clean.

After I'd washed my hands and was planning to continue working on my new series, I noticed the cats had taken their favorite spots in the apartment. Joey was on the top rung of the cat tree facing the window that looked toward Central Park. His head moved side to side as he observed a few snowflakes drifting down on the pavement below. Jake lay on the throw rug in the sitting room, curled into a striped beige and black ball of fur. Jezebel, still acting edgy, flitted about emitting short meowing noises. I interpreted this as her wanting to play. I was about to pick up one of the plastic spring coils she loved to bat under my refrigerator when my cell phone rang. Checking the display, I saw it was Laura. "Hey, Sis," I said pressing the "talk" button.

"Lily, have you seen the news?"

"No. I've only been up a short time. Am I missing something?"

"Haven't you even checked twitter or Facebook?" She sounded anxious, but I was used to her dramatics.

"I haven't. Why?" Then I thought of her husband and my niece and asked, "Is everything okay? Are Todd and Kerri alright?"

"Yes, for now, but we're all in danger. For Pete's sake, Lily, turn on the news or log into twitter. It's all over the place. They're invading. They've already destroyed the West Coast."

My heart began to race. Were terrorists at it again? I was only ten when the Twin Towers were attacked in 9/11, but I still remember that day that my father perished. Laura was eight and took it even worse than I did. She cried for weeks along with my mother. I was only able to shed tears at the funeral. We were among the lucky ones who had a body to bury.

"Lily, are you there? Have you looked?"

"Hold on, Laura." My hands were shaking as I went to my laptop and clicked on the news. The page was flooded with stories. There were YouTube videos showing decimated cities and towns. Even though all the buildings stood, bodies littered the sidewalks. Words flashed over the screen – Surprise Attack by Aliens Blasts West Coast– Millions Suspected dead. Europe and Asia Unresponsive. Major Internet Hubs Down. NASA tracking hundreds of spaceships orbiting Earth. President Young is holding a press conference at 4:30 p.m. Eastern time to discuss counter measures."

"Lily . . . Do you see? I'm so afraid." My sister's voice came through my cell. Joey and Jake, sensing the anxious atmosphere, ran and hid under my bed. Only Jezebel joined me by my laptop, her green eyes staring at the screen and the images of horror flashing across it.

"Yes, Laura, I'm here. I feel like this is a bad dream. Why are we being targeted, and where did these aliens come from?" This was worse than terrorists. How could we deal with creatures from another planet?

"Lily, I've asked Todd to load up the car. We're coming over there to be with you. We'll bring Kerri. We'll be there before the president's broadcast. We can watch it together."

"What about Mom?" I knew she'd taken a trip to visit our aunt in San Francisco.

Laura let out a sob. "I don't know. I can't reach her. This is a nightmare."

"Calm down, Laura. It'll be okay, but I don't want you coming here. I'll come to you. I'll take the train."

"What will you do with your cats? How can you bring them on the train and through the subway? I'm sure there are delays."

"I'll find a way. Don't worry."

"I can't just sit here and wait, Lily. I'm trying to stay calm for Kerri. She doesn't know what's going on. She's the same age as I was when, you know, when . . ." her voice broke.

"Just sit tight, Laura. I'll get there as soon as I can. We need to be together."

"Please hurry, Lily." Her words drowned out as my cell phone died. It wasn't the battery. I'd been charging it all night. The display read, "No Service." My laptop screen had gone blank, too. A message flashed across it. "No Internet connection."

"Oh, My God," I thought, *"We've lost internet."*

"What am I going to do?" I asked aloud. "I have to reach my sister, but I also need to bring my cats." Jezebel turned her eyes from my blank laptop and gave me that gaze I recognized. I could hear her in my head, *"Your cat club friends will help. Call them."*

Hope surged through me. "That's it, Jezzy. You're so smart." I petted her head and gave her a quick kiss on top. Then I jumped off the bed to grab the phone on the kitchen wall. I pushed away the fear that the landlines would be down, too. I was relieved to hear a dial tone. I called Amanda first. She was the secretary of our club and my veterinarian. The phone rang several times without an answer before I remembered that I was calling her cell. I had her landline number in my contacts, but I couldn't view the list. Joey and Jake joined Jezebel circling around me. They'd sensed my fear. All three tails were fat, and their ears were pointed back. Two sets of yellow eyes and Jezzy's set of green were open wide staring at me. "It's okay," I assured them, trying to calm myself. "We'll figure something out." Then what I might've considered divine intervention occurred. Loud tapping sounded at my door, and I heard Amanda's voice. "Lily, are you there? Open up." But, when I slid back the deadbolt and opened the door, it wasn't just Amanda on my step. Behind her stood the other members of the cat club; Valerie Conner, the psychologist and pet behaviorist, and Norman Baxter, the scientist. Amanda and Valerie carried cat carriers. Norman, who'd lost his only cat recently, held his hands behind his back.

As I let them in, my three cats gathered around the carriers that were deposited by my door. Yowls of greeting echoed from them. Tails still stiff, Joey, Jake, and Jezebel sniffed the boxes.

Amanda said, "I assume you've seen the news. Isn't it awful? I tried to call you, but the cell phones aren't working and I didn't have your landline."

"Same here," I said. "You've brought your cats."

"We have to get out of the city," Norman said. "That's where they'll attack first."

"I wanted to try to get to my sister's, but I can't manage three cat carriers by myself."

"That's what I figured. I can carry two," Norman offered.

"But what about your families? Shouldn't you be with them?" I'd known the members of the cat club for two years but still didn't know much about their backgrounds. Valerie and Amanda lived alone in the city except for their cats. Norman was on his own, too. The three, like me, spent most of their hours at work. We met once a month at a local cat café and played games such as Cat-o-poly, a spinoff of Monopoly, or just discussed our cats and showed one another photos and videos of them we'd taken with our iPhones. I was president because I'd established the club. Amanda Miller, my vet, was the one I'd approached with the idea first. She knew Valerie and Norman and invited them. It seemed like a nice way to share our love of felines, and the four of us became friends.

"Norman thinks there's a connection between the invasion and cats," Valerie said.

"What do you mean?"

Norman replied, "Did you see the videos of the West Coast before the Internet crashed?"

"I did. It was awful. Everyone was dead."

"Yes, everyone except the cats."

"I don't understand. I didn't notice the cats."

Amanda smiled. "That surprises me. We all seem to zero in on cats when they're in pictures or on a screen."

Before I could reply, Norman continued, "Those people weren't shot down. There was a cloud that enveloped them. Some sort of chemical or toxic agent was emitted from the ships. But, somehow, it didn't affect the cats."

Jezebel flashed me a message as she tapped her paw into the cage holding Amanda's cat, Charlie. *"He's right. We're immune."*

Valerie said, "Norman thinks if we put our heads together, we can figure out what's protecting the cats and come up with something that can help people."

"And how do you suppose we do that?" I asked, looking from Valerie to Norman.

Amanda was the one who answered. "We need to watch the president's broadcast and see what he's suggesting."

"But the Internet's down. I was planning to hear the broadcast with my sister at her house if her TV is working." Laura was one of the few people who still owned a television set. Most people watched the news and shows on their computers or phones.

"Where does she live?" Amanda asked.

"On Long Island in Hicksville. It's about an hour's drive from here but could be much longer with traffic. I thought the train would be quicker. I doubt any of you have cars, anyway."

Norman nodded. "We'll go with you to your sister's. I'll help you carry your cats."

"I can help you get them in their carriers," Amanda offered. "In my experience, it's much easier getting them in than getting them out."

I knew what she meant. Jezebel and Jake actually liked traveling in their carriers, and Joey didn't put up too much of a fuss. The trick was to be quick and leave the cases out in plain sight for a day before using them. I hadn't had time to do that, but I rushed into my bedroom where I'd stacked the three carriers. They were plastic and featured dual openings in the top and front which made it easier to get the cats inside.

As I'd expected, Jezebel and Jake went right to the boxes when I brought them out, sniffing them and peeking inside. Joey ran, but

Norman caught him and helped me slide him inside a carrier and latch the door.

"Thanks," I said. "I think we should get going. Laura must be worried since we lost communication on our cells. The landlines are still working, but I'd rather just go over there. With people panicking and trying to reach their own families, it might take some time."

"The trains are still running," Valerie said, "but I'm sure they're packed."

"Even more reason to get on the road," Norman acknowledged. He stepped over to me and took Joey's cat carrier in his left hand and Jake's case in his right. I was left with Jezebel who was meowing softly and sending me another message, "*Go . . . Go . . . Go, and don't forget your laptop*."

Besides their cat carriers, I noticed my three friends were also carrying backpacks. "What should I bring?" I asked. I felt like I wouldn't get a chance to come back again. Luckily, my mother had most of my belongings at her house. The thought of her brought a twinge of sadness to my heart.

"I only brought money, some of my clothes, and my pet first aid kit along with my uniform," Amanda said. "It's humbling to know how little we actually need."

"Then I'll get my computer, clothes, and purse." I rushed down the hall to my bedroom, stuffed my laptop in its computer bag into my backpack along with a few clothes and threw it and my purse over my shoulders. My hands were free to carry Jezebel's case.

"All ready," I said rejoining my fellow cat lovers. It felt like we were now a band of desperados.

Norman nodded. "I have a train schedule, if it's running on time, that is." He glanced at my wall clock. His Apple Watch had powered down with the Internet outage. "I think we can make the 1:45."

The cats were growing impatient. A chorus of meows bellowed from the six boxes. Jake seemed to be leading the sextet. Valerie's two Scottish fold brothers, Biscuit and Cookie, yowled in unison as if singing a duet. Amanda's Charlie was the quietest, emitting intermittent meows. Jezebel, the only female feline among the group and the single telepath as far as I knew, was growling.

I locked my apartment on the way out wondering if I'd ever set foot in it again. Stepping into the hall, I noticed an eerie quiet. Most of my neighbors had already fled. The four of us left the apartment. It was bitter cold out, and I was glad I'd placed gloves in my coat pocket. I donned them as we joined the crowds walking head down against the cold. I was reminded of the photos I'd seen nearly thirty years ago of the throngs of people escaping the city with the smoke billowing behind them from the Twin Tower blazes.

"You okay?" Norman asked, noticing my silence, although no one else was making a sound, not even the cats.

"Yes. Thank you. Are you sure you can handle both those cases?" Joey and Jake, as well as the other cats, had simmered down once they were in motion.

"They're light. If Fred was still here, it would be another story."

I heard the sadness in his voice when he spoke of his red male tabby who'd reminded me of Garfield, the cartoon cat. He'd even enjoyed a few strands of spaghetti on occasion. It wasn't true that there were only cat ladies. Many men were feline aficionados, and Norman had been one of the biggest.

"Sorry," I said. "I know you still miss him."

He nodded, a few gray hairs whipping off his face by the wind. He pulled up his collar. Forty-five and single with a rash of broken relationships behind him, we'd dated a few times but mutually agreed that our friendship was more valuable than ruining it by sleeping together.

"We only have a few minutes," he said, changing the subject. It was hard to keep up a fast pace and stay together with so many bodies around us.

When we finally caught sight of the train station, the line for tickets was mobbed. "This will take forever," Valerie sighed. "They should just let us all through."

Amanda said, "They need to ticket us to find out where we're going. We're lucky the trains are still running, or we'd be hoofing it across the bridge."

As we waited in line, the cats started acting up again, but then Jezebel sent them all a message that was carried on a loud yowl: *"Shush down, guys. We have to get out of here."* I wondered if I was wrong and that the other cats were telepaths, too, although Joey and Jake had never communicated with me. I was sure the three of them communicated with one another. Somehow, Jezebel was able to add me into the loop.

Jezebel's warning seemed to do the trick. The cats were quiet again and, after what seemed like hours, the four of us and the cats were crunched, standing, in a train section along with desperate looking people carrying their own pets, including some dogs on leashes and a parrot in a cage. Unlike our group, many lugged rolling suitcases that took up standing area or seat spaces.

"Do you believe this?" Valerie sighed again. "Some folks are just so inconsiderate of others."

I had no comment. As the train jostled on the tracks, I held on to the pole. Valerie held on to the other side. When we arrived at the Hicksville station, a swarm of people pushed forward. I went with the tide, keeping an eye out for my friends. We all ended up on the platform.

"I guess we should flag a taxi," Norman said, "if my phone was working, I could've used the Uber app."

"My sister's not far," I said, noting the huge line of people crowding the taxi stands. "I think we can walk."

We bundled into our coats. Valerie unzipped her backpack and removed a white, Cossack-like hat that she placed on her head. Amanda put up her coat's hood. I didn't have a hood on my coat or a hat. Neither did Norman, so the two of us lowered our heads into our collars. I led the way to Laura's house. She and Todd bought the three-bedroom ranch five years ago in the hope of enrolling Kerri in a good elementary school in the suburbs. I visited them for holidays and had been there recently for Christmas. Mother had joined us, and Laura had served a delicious turkey dinner. I'd brought dessert and Mother a bottle of wine that she practically consumed all by herself. Since she lost our father in 9/11, she'd been an on again, off again alcoholic.

Weighed down by the cat cases, it took us about an hour to walk the three miles to Morrison Drive, the cul-de-sac around which Laura and her family lived. The cats had kept quiet for most of the trip but, when we got close, Jezebel let out another remark attached to a yowl. *"Thank Bastet we're almost there. Move faster, Lily. I'm so cramped in this cage."*

"Laura's house is that one at the end, the tan one with the cream shutters," I said. It was close to 4 p.m. and already starting to grow dark. As I walked up the drive with my friends, I wondered how Laura would take to my bringing three other people and four cats to her door. I needn't have worried. My sister was already standing in the doorway. As soon as she saw me, she rushed out without a coat. "Oh, Lily, Oh, God. It's so good to see you." Tears streamed down her cheeks. Hugging me, I noticed the small bump that she announced at Christmas as my forthcoming niece or nephew. Standing on my tip toes because I was several inches taller than her, she looked over my shoulder at those I'd brought along.

"Sorry to spring my friends and their cats on you," I explained in a rush of words.

She shook her head and smiled, releasing me and wiping her tears away with the sleeve of her sweater. "The more the merrier. Come on in, all of you. It's cold outside. You're just in time to hear the president's Broadcast. I don't know how they managed it, but it's coming through our TV. Todd has it set up in the den."

I was shocked at how calm she was behaving now. Maybe it was the fact that I'd made it to her, or possibly she was placing hope in the president or faith in God. She'd always been more religious than me, attending church each Sunday with our parents until father's untimely death. I'd always been the one who came down with a sudden stomach ache or a last-minute school report that I wasn't planning on writing, anyway. I'd always felt guilty and a bit jealous afterwards when they came home looking so peaceful. Now I wished I'd gone with them before my mother stopped going so I could have someone to pray to, too.

Inside Laura's cozy house, I heard the TV pre-broadcasting the upcoming speech. I made the quick introductions, and Laura suggested we leave the cats with Kerri who was upstairs in her bedroom playing a DVD game. They had their own cat, Garfield, an orange tabby named by Kerri. She'd gotten him for her eighth birthday and was keeping him with her in her room.

"I hope the cats will all get along," I said.

"Maybe you should keep them in their cages," Valerie suggested.

"I don't think that's a good idea," Amanda said. "I can stay with them. You can all fill me in on what I miss."

"Are you sure?" I asked.

"Yes. I'm a vet. I can ease any tension that arises among the cats, and I can keep Kerri company."

I knew that Amanda, who ran a cat-only practice and was active in cat rescue, had lost her own daughter and husband in a tragic car crash three years ago when they were coming home from a dance recital that Amanda couldn't attend because of an emergency at her cat clinic. Amanda's daughter had been eight at the time of her death, the same age as Kerri.

Laura knew Amanda's story. "Thanks, Amanda," she said. "Kerri will love to meet you. She told me she'd like to be a veterinarian when she grows up. I know she's young and her plans may change, but I'm sure she'll have lots of questions for you about what you do."

"I'll be happy to answer them," she said, placing her hand on the stairway rail and holding Charlie's carrier in the other. "No need to bring me up, I'll just follow the sound of the game."

"I can bring the other cats up," Norman offered.

"You'd have to make a few trips," I said. "I'll bring Jezebel. Valerie, you give me your carriers. I can carry two." I made the offer, so I could say hello to Kerri.

"Thank you," Laura said, "but don't take too long. The broadcast is about to start. Meet us in the den. I've put out the muffins Kerri and I baked, and I'll make tea and coffee if anyone wants some."

Up in Kerri's room, Norman dropped the cat carriers inside the door and I placed Jezebel's by the bed. Kerri sat on it stroking Garfield who probably reminded Norman of his lost cat. Her notebook computer lay by her side flashing a computer game featuring the characters from Frozen V, but she wasn't playing.

"Hi, Kerri," I said. "I've brought my cats, and my friends Amanda and Norman have brought three others. I hope Garfield doesn't mind them joining him. Amanda is a vet and will help get them acquainted."

"Aunt Lily," Kerri said, jumping off the bed and running to hug me. "Will you stay and play with me?"

"I'm sorry, honey. I have to go downstairs with your mom and dad. We're watching an important show, but I'll come right back up here and play with you later. Okay?"

She pulled away, a frown replacing her smile. "Why can't I watch the show, too?"

Amanda stepped into the room. Norman remained by the door. I could tell he was eager to get downstairs, or maybe seeing Garfield was affecting him.

"I'll play with you now, Kerri. I'll also answer any questions you have about being a vet. I heard that you'd like to be one when you grow up."

Kerri's blue eyes grew wide. With her blonde curls and fair skin, she was a mini version of Laura. I'd been the one to inherit my father's darker coloring.

"I would love that," she said. "I'd rather talk to you than play a computer game, but can we play doctor with the cats? I have a kit." She ran over to her closet and started rummaging through her toy shelf.

"I have a real kit," Amanda said. "It's here in my backpack." She dropped the bag to the floor.

"Looks like you ladies will be occupied," Norman said. "Let's leave them and go hear what the president has to say."

I turned to him. "See you later, Kerri. Thanks, Amanda."

As I left the room, Jezebel sent me another message. "*You didn't thank me. I'm keeping these cats in control. The vet can't handle them the way I can. But I know how you can make it up to me. Those chicken treats you packed in your backpack with some of our cans would do the trick.*" I ignored her and followed Norman downstairs.

Norman and I took a seat in the fold-up chairs Todd had placed facing the TV. We were just in time as the president began her address. Everyone was quiet as we entered the room, their eyes riveted on the screen.

"Good morning," newly elected President Samantha Young, said. Her tone was somber, but the words that followed gave us hope. "I know you have all been awaiting news about the alien attack that has taken place today. It was unexpected and frightening. For those with families and friends on the West Coast or in other countries, I have some good news." She took a breath, her dark eyes staring toward the screen. "I have confirmation that there have been no casualties. The attack wasn't aimed at killing anyone. Our West Coast and international friends and family are alive but asleep. I've had communication from the aliens who speak our language and many others. I will play that recording for you now." She paused. I held my breath as she tapped a button on a device on her desk, and I was sure everyone in the room was doing the same.

The voice that came through had no accent but sounded robotic. It was a woman's voice speaking in a monotone. "Hello Madam President. My name is Catling. I am the leader of my planet Felinedae in a Solar System light years away from your Earth. We are not here to harm your people. We apologize for sending them into deep sleep. We thought it was the best way to proceed with our mission without being deterred. We will wake them soon, and they will remember nothing about seeing or hearing us. But we've decided that we should communicate with the leaders of your world to explain our mission. I've chosen you, Madam President, to contact first." There was a buzzing sound as the recording paused for a few seconds. I was still breathing shallowly. It seemed unreal, hearing a message from an alien from another world, but it wasn't unlike when I heard Jezebel in my head for the first time.

Catling continued, "Our mission is simple. We merely want to collect some items we sent down to Earth ages ago. These items have served to retrieve data about your world. They are now needed back on Felinedae as our experiment is complete, and they must be sent to another planet for our continued research. I refer to the animals and pets you call "cats." Our programming has survived through each generation in our special DNA, although only a certain percentage of the felines retain it. We can pinpoint these animals and will send down retrieval parties to bring them home. We only ask that you allow this without standing in our way. If any of you do, we will be forced to take more serious measures. You may already know that we have spaceships circling your planet and will begin our retrieval missions by setting them down in the locations where our cats are located within sixty of your minutes after this communication and hope to complete the retrievals around your world within twenty-four hours. Thank you for your compliance." The recording ended. President Young raised her eyebrows. "This recording has been shared with the ASPCA and animal welfare organizations. I have two cats myself. Measures will be taken to ensure the safety of all pets."

A flood of questions was directed at the president by the press covering the broadcast, but she couldn't answer most of them. I was still in shock. Could Jezebel, with her telepathic powers, be one of the cats from this distant planet? Could I give her up if it meant my life otherwise? I loved all my cats and the only decision I thought I'd face one day was euthanizing them.

"Do you think they'll take Garfield?" Laura asked. "Kerri would be heartbroken."

"No one is taking my boys," Valerie said.

"I can't part with any of my cats either," I said.

"This is the only time I'm glad to be without a pet," Norman added. "I wonder what type of measures the president is proposing. She didn't specify. The Felinedaens must be an advanced race, and if what this being Catling says is true, they have knowledge about our world that would render useless any tactics we employ. I know it all sounds unbelievable, but from my experience with cats, I'm not shocked. I've always found them to be intuitive, and there's no denying that they have a knack for winning people over with their intelligence and beauty."

"We must be able to do something," Valerie said. "We should run it by Amanda. She's worked with cats for over twenty years."

I was compelled to tell them about Jezebel, but I was afraid to share our secret even with my cat club friends.

"I'll go up and ask her to come down," I said. "I promised Kerri that I'd play a game with her when we were done watching the show."

"I'll start dinner," Laura said. "I know you all must be hungry after your travels. We don't have many extra rooms here, but I could double up with Lily. Norman can stay in the den with Todd, and Valerie and Amanda could sleep with Kerri. Would that be okay?"

"What about the cats?" Valerie asked.

"They can stay in Kerri's room, too. I have extra cat food and also an extra litter box. I keep one in each bathroom. The cats can use the one upstairs."

"You've thought of everything," I said, relieved that we would all be able to stick together.

Upstairs, I found Amanda and Kerri grooming the cats. Kerri was brushing Garfield from his head down to his tail as he purred. Amanda had the two Scottish fold cats next to her, gliding a cat comb through each one. I had a hard time telling which was Cookie and which was Biscuit, but I was sure Valerie had no problem recognizing them. Jezebel sat on the floor by Charlie as they waited their turns to be groomed. As soon as I entered, Jezebel got up and padded over to me. *"It's about time you're back. Fill me in on what's going on."*

"You tell me," I signaled to her in my mind, *"You've been sending messages to another world, and now your people will be picking you up."*

"I know nothing about that," she replied, raising her tail high and stalking away across the bedroom.

Amanda looked up and smiled. "Jezebel seemed to miss you, but now she's ignoring you. Typical feline behavior." When she noticed my expression, she put the combs down. Biscuit and Cookie were already dozing and didn't seem to mind. "Kerri, I think I should talk to your aunt. Do you mind if we leave you for a minute? You can finish grooming the cats. It's Charlie and Jezebel's turns next."

Kerri pouted. "No. I want to hear what happened. Why is everyone so afraid of telling me?"

I remembered being just a few years older than her when our mother broke the news to me and Laura that our father had died in the terrorist attack on 9/11. I didn't know how Laura wanted to handle telling Kerri that her cat might be taken away to another planet.

"I'll speak to your mother," I said. "She should be the one to explain everything to you."

Kerri nodded. "Okay. I think she'll listen to you, Aunt Lily."

Amanda and I stepped out of the room. I turned to her in the hall and whispered, "I think it's better you watch a replay of the Broadcast. I'm sure there'll be a few of them before midnight."

"No, Ms. Palmer. You're not getting away that easy." Amanda's green eyes, so like Jezebel's, widened. "Spill it."

I continued to whisper. "I don't want Kerri to hear. If Laura decides to tell her, that's different. It's about the cats."

"What?"

"The president played a recording of the alien leader's communication. The good news is that everyone is alive but in a deep sleep. They're going to wake them up. The aliens don't mean us harm."

"Then why did they attack? I don't understand, and what do you mean it's about the cats?"

I paused, lowering my voice another octave and hoping Kerri wasn't pressing her ear against the wall to hear our words. "I know this sounds strange, but this alien calling herself Catling claimed that they sent a bunch of cats to Earth a long time ago to monitor and record our habits. They now want to collect these cats, or the ones descended from them, so they can send them to another world."

Amanda laughed, but it was a short, dry giggle. "This is unbelievable. I've got to go downstairs and see that replay for myself."

"I told you."

"What does Dr. Baxter think?"

"Norman seems intrigued, but you have to remember he has no pets right now."

"So, he's taking this serious?"

I nodded. "Yes. I'm afraid so. Why don't you go downstairs and talk to him? Ask Laura to come up here for a minute. I'll stay with Kerri and the cats until she gets here."

"Will do," Amanda said. "This is freaking weird," she muttered more to herself than to me. "It's almost as odd as finding a decent heterosexual single guy over forty in New York."

I laughed at her remark, even though I felt the same. She'd introduced me to many online dating sites including those for widows and widowers that she said I might find a good man on. Both of us had given up after meeting a bunch of losers. I often wondered why she didn't make a play for Norman, but I figured there wasn't an attraction between them. I had to admit that Norman was more my type. Valerie didn't have anyone special in her life either, but she'd been open with us about her sexual orientation and that she was seeking a nice woman to marry.

Laura agreed that Kerri should know the truth, and she spoke to her daughter alone. When I went to check on them, Kerri was sobbing in her mother's arms. "I don't want them to take Garfield. Please can we hide him?"

"They may not want him, sweetie. But if they do, we have to let him go. I'm so sorry. We'll get another cat."

She sniffled as I walked in. "Aunt Lily. Can you do anything? Are they going to take your cats, too?"

"I have no idea," I said, although I suspected Jezebel would be the one they'd want. She was strangely silent as I entered the room. Suddenly, outside, there was a whirring sound, like the propellers of a helicopter. All the cats' ears perked up, and they ran to the window. Kerri had a multi-level cat tree in front of it. Jezebel pushed the others away as she climbed to the highest level. Cookie and Biscuit both grabbed the middle level. Charlie, Jake, and Joey all crunched together on the bottom while Garfield gazed up crying because there was no room for him. Kerri raced to the window. Amanda and I followed. The sight we saw was incredible. A bright spotlight shone in a circle so intense I was afraid to look at it directly or it might harm my eyes as I worried about what might happen to my cats when I played with laser toys with them. A huge spaceship was landing in Laura and Todd's backyard.

"Oh, my God!" Laura exclaimed. "They're here to pick up the cats."

"No!" Kerri yelled grabbing Garfield and running from the room. Laura and I ran after her down the stairs. "Todd, get Kerri," Laura yelled catching her breath from behind me. But the others were still in the TV room down the hall talking. I wasn't sure whether they'd seen or heard the spaceship landing. I had no time to find out because Kerri had already run out the door. I raced after her and through the front gate that opened into the backyard. "*Slow down,*" I heard a voice behind me. It was Jezebel, not Laura. She must've jumped off the cat tree and run after us.

I wondered why Kerri was running to the spaceship instead of away from it. My unspoken question was answered when Kerri stopped a few feet from the ship and yelled, "If you want Garfield, you will have to take me, too. He's my friend. I won't leave him with you."

The spacecraft's hatch opened to reveal a six-foot cat standing on two legs. "We don't want your cat," the alien said. "We want the other one." She pointed a long paw in my direction. I realized it was aimed at Jezebel.

It was my turn to argue with this creature who wanted to take away my pet. "You can't have her either," I said scooping Jezebel into my arms.

I turned to Kerri next to me. "Go back in the house with your mom and the others. I can handle this."

Kerri seemed unsure, but then she turned and ran to the house holding Garfield. Laura waited in the doorway. I saw the others gathered around her watching. Todd and Norman ran over to us. Both men carried guns. I forgot that my brother-in-law had a license to keep them for protection.

The alien said, "Those weapons are useless against me. Drop them and leave the cat, or I will have to retaliate."

"Don't shoot," I told the men. I was hoping Jezebel would tell me what to do, but she was silent as a normal cat except for her enlarged tail as she gazed at the creature in the doorway and hissed.

"If my cat is one that you said you're using for research purposes, why is she reacting that way?" I asked.

"As part of this project, the cats who were recruited were not aware of their participation. We are able to telepathically receive communication from them. It's time for another project."

"Well, that's great," I exclaimed. "but how many of these cats do you need? What difference will it make if one stays here?"

The alien laughed, a mechanical sound that filled the cold, nighttime air. Todd and Norman still had their guns aimed at her. "I'm sure all you Earthlings will want us to forget your pets but that's not possible. Hand her over, or there will be consequences."

Jezebel paused in her hissing and sent an urgent message on a yowl. *"I won't go with you. I want to stay with Lily."*

I picked her up and cuddled her against my chest. "Don't worry, Jezzy," I promised aloud. "You aren't going anywhere. I love you, and Joey and Jake would miss you very much."

My heart beat fast as I feared the alien's retaliation. The others were looking on in fear. Kerri was still crying.

Todd and Norman took a step closer to me. I knew that if the alien tried to hurt me, they'd do what they could to protect me. It was then that I realized a cloud of smoke was gathering around the spaceship and spreading over the backyard and into the house. I began to cough, and so did Todd and Norman. I heard the others coughing from the door. Jezebel said, *"She's putting you all into deep sleep, so they can take me. Goodbye, Lily. Thank you for being such a wonderful human mom to me."*

As I released Jezebel and fell to the ground, my last thought was that I would never see her again.

My head was fuzzy, and there was something pressing on my stomach. I opened my eyes to see Jezebel kneading the blanket over my middle. *"Wake up, Sleepyhead. I'm starving."* She glared at me, as I heard her thoughts in my mind. Then she jumped off the bed and ran toward the kitchen.

Still in a fog, as if I'd been drugged, I glanced around the room My laptop lay next to me with a Word document open to the page I was starting on my new book. The time clock on my computer read 7 p.m. How could that be? I'd lost a whole day. Had I nodded off to sleep after finishing the *Booklist* review? I'd never done anything like that in my life, although I remembered having a few glasses of wine with the book club members the night before when I had them over for dinner. Suddenly, a pop-up window appeared at the bottom of my screen from Facebook, "Breaking News." I clicked it open and read a strange report from Washington, D.C. "The animal shelters and rescues across the country are overwhelmed tonight with calls and appearances by people who claim their cats have disappeared." I scrolled down the page to see similar stories published by local and international news. Finding a video, I clicked to watch one from here in New York. A crying woman was being interviewed about her cat. "I don't know what happened to Kitty," she sniffled. "I woke up, and she was gone. Kitty's an indoor cat. I never let her out, and I never fall asleep that early. I think someone broke in, roofied me, and stole my cat."

I wanted to read the rest, but I heard Jezebel yowling near her food bowl. As I got out of bed, dizzily, I realized I was fully dressed. I could've sworn I'd been in my pajamas while I was working on the review. I also noticed my backpack was on a chair by the bed. I always stored it in my closet and only took it out when I went on an overnight trip to my sister's house. I wanted to explore more to figure out this puzzle, but Jezebel's demanding meows were increasing the pounding in my head.

I went to the kitchen where she sat by the bowls. I filled them all up with kibble, canned food, and water. *"About time,"* she telepathed digging into the food.

I looked around. "Where are Joey and Jake?" I asked aloud. The boys usually came running as soon as they heard me put out the cat food.

Jezebel paused in her munching. *"Oh, they took a little trip, Lily, but don't worry. They'll be back in a few months and when they come home, you'll be able to converse with them like you do with me."* In a lower voice that I could hardly hear, she added, *"So glad I was able to convince Catling that she should collect more data using unbiased sources.*

She said it wouldn't take too long to train those boys. In the meantime, I can have all the kibble and Lily all to myself. It was a nice surprise that those Felinedaens also know how to teleport. I certainly hated that train ride and being enclosed in my box so long."

About Debbie De Louise

Debbie De Louise is an award-winning author and a reference librarian at a public library on Long Island. She is a member of Sisters-in-Crime, International Thriller Writers, the Long Island Authors Group, and the Cat Writers' Association. Her novels include the five books and three stories of the Cobble Cove cozy mystery series, a comedy novella, When Jack Trumps Ace, a paranormal romance, Cloudy Rainbow, and the standalone mysteries; Reason to Die, Sea Scope, and Memory Makers. Her latest book, Pet Posts: The Cat Chats is a non-fiction pet book. Debbie has also written three short eBooks featuring the Cobble Cove characters: Celebrating Christmas with my Characters, Sneaky's Christmas Mystery (the 2019 MUSE Medallion winner from the Cat Writers' Association) and Sneaky's Summer Mystery. She lives on Long Island with her husband, Anthony; daughter, Holly; and 3 cats Stripey, Harry, and Hermione.

Also by Debbie De Louise

The Cobble Cove mystery series:

A Stone's Throw

Between a Rock and a Hard Place

Written in Stone

Love on the Rocks

No Gravestone Unturned

The standalone mysteries:

Reason to Die

Sea Scope

Memory Makers.

The romantic comedy novella:

When Jack Trumps Ace

The paranormal romance

Cloudy Rainbow

Non-fiction

Pet Posts: The Cat Chats

Contact Debbie de Louise

Facebook: https://www.facebook.com/debbie.delouise.author/

Twitter: https://twitter.com/Deblibrarian

Goodreads: https://www.goodreads.com/author/show/2750133.Debbie_De_Louise

Amazon Author Page: http://amzn.to/2bIHdaQ

All Author: https://allauthor.com/author/debbiedelouise/

Instagram: https://www.instagram.com/debbie_writer/

Linkedin: https://www.linkedin.com/in/debbiedelouise/

Bookbub: https://www.bookbub.com/profile/debbie-de-louise

Pinterest: https://www.pinterest.com/debbiedelouise

Debbie's Character's Chat Group: https://www.facebook.com/groups/748912598599469/

Website/Blog/Newsletter Sign-Up: https://debbiedelouise.com

Sneaky the Library Cat's blog: https://Sneakylibrarycat.wordpress.com

PART III

A Trip for The Books

Adventure with our writers on this edition of ***The Red Penguin Collection*** as we travel the globe on "A Trip For The Books". In this anthology of travel-inspired works, you will quickly find yourself swept up by stories of great journeys, trials on the road, and destinations that made it all worthwhile. From Africa to Mexico, Disney World to the Australian Outback, our esteemed authors are prepared to share with you their most memorable tales. The spirit of adventure awaits!

1

The Spomenik Tales

SHANNON FROST GREENSTEIN

PROLOGUE: PODGARIC

My grandfather was nearly tortured to death in 1944.

I don't know *why* he was tortured–if he was privy to some super-secret information, or if he was just captured by a particularly sadistic Fascist–but he apparently lasted for several days before he was rescued and delivered to a field hospital in Serbia.

I don't know why I'm telling you this.

It's just, it's hard to grow up with that fact as part of your genetic blueprint, as the framework for your nuclear family, the Ice-Nine upon which generation after generation is built. It's hard when that's your origin story, you know? It's hard to live up to.

My grandfather was a potato farmer, if you can believe it; he did nothing but farm potatoes his whole life, until the war came. Then he joined the Workers' Battalion in Serbia during the Battle of Kadinjaca, only it was still Yugoslavia back then. He was tortured and rescued and healed, and then returned to life as usual, raising my father and giving my grandmother gifts on their anniversary for the next 40 years. My family didn't even emigrate from Eastern Europe until right before the Yugoslav Wars in the 90s.

He died a few months after he arrived in the United States with my grandmother and my parents. He went to see the *Spomeniks* before they left, when he knew he would never be back to Serbia; it was the most significant thing, he said on his deathbed, that he did in this life.

I was born about a year later, and *that's* the opening act I had to follow.

I'm babbling, aren't I? Forgive me. It's just, finally being here, finally starting, is making me a little giddy; I've been planning this for so long. You get it, I hope.

Anyway, the only photograph we have of my grandfather, the tattered, sun-bleached portrait that accompanied my family as they fled from Serbia to Philadelphia, hangs right above our fireplace. I see it every morning when I wake up, and every evening as I go to bed. It's like he's watching everything I do. I feel like he's my yardstick; in life; in everything.

I feel like I've never measured up.

I guess that's why I'm on this trip. After I dropped out of school, after my parents ended my tenure in my childhood bedroom, I immediately started to plan to come to my grandfather's birthplace in Croatia. I'm going to Serbia, to the site of the Battle of Kadinjaca. I've come to do exactly as my grandfather did, to stop at as many of the *Spomeniks* as possible, to follow his route and hopefully, to live as he lived. If I walk in his footsteps, travel the ground he walked, see the things he saw, maybe I could somehow come away from this more like him, thanks to sheer proximity; maybe it will rub off on me like pollen.

Maybe I'll leave with some of his legendary work ethic, or his oft-mentioned integrity, or his natural leadership. Maybe the land itself will force me to evolve like Galapagos did Darwin's finches; maybe it will infuse me with my grandfather's strength through osmosis. Maybe I'll finally grow up, or discover something meaningful about myself, or just be…be *better*, you know? Better.

I'm totally babbling. I can hear it.

But I don't *mean* to smoke so much pot all the time. I don't mean to keep getting fired. I'm always, always trying my best, but I'm always coming up short; and to think that my grandfather was tortured for days while I can't even get a Bachelor's degree is completely unacceptable.

Anyway. This trip is going to change things. I'm sure of it.

Thanks for agreeing to come along.

THE PILGRIMMAGE

Podgaric was anticlimactic.

I mean, I guess I shouldn't be so harsh about it. It was big, and it looked cool, and it photographed well, but I didn't feel any different being there, you know? I thought I would feel like I do in church, or I would suddenly understand what makes people go to war, or I would learn precisely what to do to make my father proud, but literally none of those things happened.

We're on the road today, only stopping for food and the bathroom until we get to Slabinja. I had planned to use these hours outlining everything I know about my grandfather's life, trying to find whatever it is I'm missing that makes me so pale in comparison.

I'm realizing, though, that I don't know as much about him as I thought I did, and this is surprising. My whole life, he's been this figure, this patriarch, this myth I should want to live up to but is too imposing to ever understand. But now, as I really delve into his story with nothing on my hands but time, I'm seeing all the voids in the family tales, all the patches in the storytelling I never realized covered gaping holes in my own history.

I know he was born in Podgaric somewhere around 1910; I know he had only brothers. I know he farmed potatoes and married my Grandmother in Kadinjaca and joined the resistance there when the war came. And I know he traveled from his birthplace in Croatia back to Serbia one final time in his late 70s, to see the Spomeniks; my father said he insisted on going alone.

But, I mean, that's something, right? That's at least something to go on; enough, hopefully, for a seismic personal shift.

After all, the Spomeniks mean something. They're the whole reason I'm here. The whole time I was preparing for this trip, they represented all that was good about my grandfather, and all that could be good about me; the seed of potential lodged deep within my bones. They just have to be the answer. Because…otherwise…I'll just be an out-of-work bartender who spent his life savings on a trip to Croatia and came home with nothing. To be honest, the whole thing felt so auspicious before I started; but just like with Podgaric, it's all been a bit of a letdown, so far.

If I were ever to meet my grandfather, if I were to go back in time to this very spot, if we were to meet on the road…would that be a letdown, too?

Spomenik is the Serb-Croatian word for "monument." Used collectively, the term refers to the spate of giant, brutalist, futuristic memorials which were built across the former country of Yugoslavia between the end of the second world war and the country's dissolution in the early 1990s. These architectural wonders were meant to celebrate the anti-fascist resistance of the Balkan states and commemorate those who died in the region's brutal conflicts during WWII.

While popular opinion incorrectly refers to the *Spomeniks* as "Communist War Memorials," and misinterprets them as monuments to the glory of Communism, they are in fact exactly the opposite: A celebration of Yugoslav brotherhood and unity, a rejection of Soviet influence in the post-WWII era, and a grandiose symbol of the nation's bright future.

I've heard all this from my grandmother and my parents more times than I can count; as a first-generation American, my childhood was rife with stories and practices and customs of the world that my family had left behind. My grandfather's journey among the *Spomeniks* was significant enough that it became lodged in family lore, sure to be a part of oral history for generations to come. It was why they popped into my head after I got fired for smoking pot on the clock, again, and had no earthly obligations other than continuing to disappoint my parents.

Of course, I also know that many of the *Spomeniks* my grandfather visited in the twilight of his life were damaged or destroyed when Yugoslavia fell apart at the end of the 20th century; they became unfortunate casualties of neglect and military destruction as individual countries broke away towards independence. Since then, most of those which remain have fallen victim to vandalism and disrepair. There is graffiti; corrosion; structural breakdown from the natural elements. The *Spomeniks* are, currently, abandoned orphans subject to all the injustices of being left behind.

So I'm here now, trying my best to find something I won't know I've found, because I don't know what it is. But I will know if and when I have changed, when I have surpassed myself; I will know when the *Spomeniks* have worked, like an alchemist creating something entirely new that was not there before, a better version of who I am now; creating someone like my grandfather.

This trip is my vision quest.

My grandmother never got over leaving her home and losing her husband. She is still back in Yugoslavia, frozen in the past, as her body ages in Philadelphia in real time. I used to wonder if my family's obsession with my grandfather was similar, a melancholy craving for a vestige of the old world, a bittersweet reminder of what was had and what was lost. Maybe it is not only the *Spomeniks* that have been blown out of proportion, but the life of the man himself.

But then I think about the look on my father's face when he speaks about *his* father. I think about how rarely I have seen his face do that because of me, because of things I've accomplished or summits I've reached, maybe because I've been too stoned to reach any summits; or to keep a job, even.

And then I have a moment where the only thing I want is to make my father proud, I want it all-encompassingly, I want it so much it hurts, and I resolve to quit smoking pot and start going to the gym and volunteer with the local church; anything to see that same look on my father's face and know that I, and not my grandfather's torture, have put it there.

I need this on a spiritual level, this sacred pilgrimage following in my grandfather's footsteps to a famous Mecca I've never seen. And if the *Spomeniks* are exaggerated – or, worse, meaningless? Then I guess I've got to figure out something else. Because if this doesn't mean anything…I'm nothing.

My feet hurt so badly.

I should have known that guy we picked up was bad news. I should have known never to trust him. It's just, he seemed like a good guy. He seemed genuine…like he really needed the ride, and the friends.

This is how it always happens. My entire life, my entire fucking life, is this exact scenario. I try to do good, and then I fuck up, and then I get stuck, and then I get saved somehow and the entire process starts over again.

I know, I shouldn't beat myself up like this. But, at the end of the day, it's still all on me. I was the one who said we should pick up a hitchhiker; I'm the one who let him drive, and go off to get the food; I let him out of my sight. And now, we're in the middle of nowhere and we don't have a car and I have no idea what to do next.

You're not…you're not going to go your own way, are you? I mean, you totally can, please don't think I'm stopping you, but I'm just… used to the company, I guess.

Oh, good. Thank you.

Let's just keep walking.

SLABINJA

Slabinja is pretty boring, too.

I'm shocked by how dilapidated it is. The concrete is starting to crumble away, and all of the paint has chipped on the inscriptions, and there's literal moss growing on the metal. But what's more than that is how…forgotten…it all feels.

We took the main road into Slabinja, but there are no signs that this monument exists: No blue placards, no symbol on a highway sign, nothing. And then, after what appeared to be an abandoned school, we get there, we actually drive up to this gargantuan sculpture in all its majesty, and could there be anything *more* eerie than a playground right across the street? A child's play structure, cheery reds and yellows and animals on springs, the best vantage point for the resplendently-imposing *Monument to Fallen Fighters and Victims of Fascism from Slabinja,* and I suddenly feel like I'm in a Twilight Zone episode about the fall of the USSR from the USSR's perspective.

I'm starting to worry I've made a mistake. I went through such shit to get here, and I'm going through such shit while I'm here, and I'm just not...*feeling* any different. Other than annoyed.

Oh, don't get me wrong, I'm not saying I want to go home. Like I said, I kind of need this to work out.

What's that?

Well...I guess I'm not sure *what* that would look like. Just that I'll be, intrinsically, different than I was before. Enhanced, you know? Improved. If I'm very lucky, I'll go home a fraction as charismatic and capable and...*worthy*...as my grandfather was.

Worthy of what? I don't know. That's a good question, I guess. Just worthy of the type of respect my father gave him. Worthy of being hung on a mantle. Worthy of a woman like my grandmother, and strong enough to take care of her for our whole lives.

I guess I want to be worthy of love.

I think I'm starting to fall in love.

Ever since Gornji Jelovac, *I've been…feeling things.*

It's crazy. I mean, she wasn't even supposed to be *here. I had planned to do this trip completely on my own, a prophet going into the desert for forty days; penance of sorts, or a form of absolution.*

But what are the chances of running into an old friend from camp a decade later, in fucking Croatia of all places, a friend similarly unattached and free to roam? What are the chances that this friend you've not seen since the age of 13 will have turned out to be amazingly beautiful with a great sense of humor and interesting things to say?

I'll admit, asking her on a whim to come with me to Serbia did feel slightly wrong at first; like I was cheating in my atonement, my atonement for being me.

But then we started catching up, trading the Cliffs Notes-version of our lives over the past decade since camp. I filled her ears with the mythology of my grandfather's life; she opened up about the depression that has kept her unmoored since college. We grew more comfortable, and something shifted, and now I can't stop thinking about her.

We're en route to Jasenovac, and I'm hoping this will go better than it has been, now that we have another rental car. She was even magnanimous about that, though, accepting the miles we would have to walk, cheerfully humming pop songs from the 90s and occasionally grasping my hand over rocky terrain.

I'm watching her now, as she drives. I'm typing on the notes app of my phone; I want to capture this, this moment, this feeling. I've never really felt it before. The sun is coming in through the windshield and the windows are open and she is illuminated from within, a ring of light circling her head like an aura.

I'm supposed to be thinking about my grandfather, and building my character, and filling in all the voids in my very self which make me unemployable and disagreeable and a disappointment to my father; but instead, I'm just thinking about sex.

Maybe I'll tell her all this when we get there.

JASENOVAC

Ok, this one is actually beautiful.

It looks so much better than the last few; it doesn't look like an Olympic venue from the 1980s that's been abandoned and taken over by wildflowers or rabbits or whatever.

It's called *Cvjetni Spomenik;* it means "Flower Monument." But as I wander around the museum, reading passages, glimpsing images, taking in the gestalt, I am increasingly unsettled by the cognitive dissonance between this monument's cheery name and the events which led to its construction.

Jasenovac, I learned from a handy museum flyer, was a concentration camp. Over 100,000 individuals were exterminated here by the fascist Ustasa–Croatian Revolutionary Movement before it was discovered by Partisan forces in early May of 1945. It's when I get to the part that these victims were mostly killed one-on-one, with knives or blunt objects like hammers or axes, that I put down the flyer and look out through a window towards the massive sculpture.

Jasenovac is indeed a flower in every sense of the word; it appears to have sprouted quite naturally from the ground and grown an easy 80 feet into the air. It is disorienting, its size proportionate to the amount of blood spilled at its roots. I see various earthen mounds around the base that, as the flyer has so helpfully informed me, mark where the various death camp buildings stood. I feel strange, looking up at the gargantuan petals and then down at the grass-covered hillocks, as if I've seen something I wasn't supposed to see.

This could have been my grandfather's fate, in another town, in another life.

As it stands, I wouldn't normally call anyone who has endured hours upon hours of torture "lucky," but being in a place that has witnessed so much trauma, so much death, has cowed me. My grandfather *was* fortunate, it would seem, despite the PTSD from which he suffered, the flashbacks my father would occasionally mention while reminiscing about childhood. My grandfather was lucky, because so many others–young men, just like him, with families, with plans, with potential–had not been.

I emerge from the museum and approach the monument. She is several steps ahead of me, and I notice the sunlight on her hair, the shape of her calf muscles below her sundress. Unbidden, a thought of kissing her comes to me, a thought of her kissing me back, and the sudden feeling behind my xiphoid process, deep in my chest, is so strong that I stop in my tracks for a moment.

She reaches the giant stone flower and turns around; gestures at me to join her. I resume walking, my heartbeat slightly increased at the thoughts which come after kissing, and the thoughts after that, and join her in leaning against the opulent statue.

We stay at *Jasenovac* for over two hours, exactly where we stand; we lean against the concrete until our legs tire and we sink down to sit right on the ground.

We talked. We only talked. But we really *talked.*

I think it has to be one of those universal human experiences, that first deep conversation with someone new, someone exciting, someone for whom you are starting to have feelings. We had *that* kind of a conversation, and as the sun set over *Jasenovac* and the temperature dropped and she began to hug herself against the cold, I didn't hesitate to lean over and drape my hoodie over her shoulders.

I almost kissed her. I really almost did. But at the last minute, when I was so close to her that I could see her individual eyelashes and it would have been *so easy* to lean in the rest of the way and press my lips to hers–all I could think about was my grandfather.

I mean, what was he feeling, when he stood here? My grandfather, who had already lived three full lives in the amount of time it took me to drop out of community college, what was it like for him to stand in the shadow of *Jasenovac* at the end of his life and look up to the sky, with all he had seen, with all he had experienced? I couldn't stop asking myself those questions and, as I stared into the eyes of a woman I might already love while I pretended to adjust the hoodie around her arms, I found I couldn't kiss her. I didn't feel *worthy* of kissing her.

Instead, I heard my brain reminding me again of my various failures in life, each shameful memory an indication that I do not deserve to be kissed; I saw my grandfather's portrait above the mantle, looking down on me as if just waiting for my next mistake.

I could have been kissing a girl, and I was instead letting my dead grandfather judge me, so I can't say this trip has been going perfectly. But maybe it isn't such a mistake after all. Maybe it really is my shot to make something of myself, my chance to…matter. To matter *to* someone. And maybe it'll all happen with her right by my side.

We walked back to the car after I gave her my sweatshirt. Now we're at a campsite, and I'm writing this by the light of my phone, and I'm still *kicking myself for not kissing her.*

I'm going to do it tomorrow.

KOZARA

It's called the Monument to the Revolution, and it's on top of a mountain.

We're currently in Bosnia, *Kozara* is literally on the mountain's peak, and the Monument to the Revolution is taking my breath away.

Getting here was a bitch; we drove through a bunch of nothing, and then even more nothing, and then straight up, practically, for an incredibly long time. But now we're here, and it's a pinnacle of achievement, architecture like pornography and fine art made incarnate. I feel truly dwarfed, physically and existentially, for the first time in my life.

After squashing myself deep into the monument's hollow interior, I peer up through the hole in the ceiling of the 100-foot monolith. Sunbeams are drowning the hidden space in light and shadow and I feel, in this moment, something almost hallowed. I feel like I do on the rare occasion I visit a friend's church or synagogue, that there is something sacred happening within the walls, even if I do not abscribe to any religious tenets–or God in general, come to think of it.

After all, what kind of merciful God allows someone to be tortured for days without intervening?

I sit inside the Monument to the Revolution, cloistered with my thoughts, my sense of awe. Outside, there is a memorial garden listing the names of the 9,921 Partisan fighters killed during the Kozara Offensive in 1942; many of them, apparently, peasant civilians who marched into battle unarmed. And as the sun starts to dwindle and the shadows shift and I wonder absentmindedly when I'll get the courage to kiss my traveling companion, I also wonder what it feels like to march towards certain death.

Eventually, I stand up and worm my way back out of the monolith. The sun is setting and the sky is bright with color and now is the moment, I've decided, to make a move; now is the time, because she is beautiful and I have fallen in love and I feel, suddenly, out of nowhere, *purpose*.

I walk with confident strides towards the museum where she waits, picturing her lips, for the first time experiencing what it feels like to march, not towards certain death, but towards the future.

I should have known.

I should have known she'd leave.

BRATUNAK

I'm finally at Bratunak.

I think it's ugly.

Let me explain.

It's completely derelict. The entire place looks neglected; there's graffiti everywhere. There are weeds covering literally everything, and all of the memorial plaques are damaged, and, also, she ripped my heart out and left me to die alone in Bosnia with a gaping chest wound.

I know my grandfather was tortured, but I bet even he has not known pain like this.

She had me completely fooled. We drove across Bosnia, sharing intimate details, having sex, sleeping together beneath the stars. I felt like I had found something precious, the missing puzzle piece to precisely fill my empty half.

And then…this morning…I woke up and she was just…gone. Actually, it wasn't just that she was gone, it was that every trace of her had disappeared; it was as if she had never existed. Her empty water bottles, the ends of the joints we smoked, the tops of discarded condom wrappers… everything that could prove I had shared a few days with a woman who stole my heart was gone. And now it's just me, heartless.

This entire travesty was almost starting to seem worthwhile. I was learning about the history of my homeland; I was starting to feel… transformed here. I was starting to feel a calling, driven from within, stirred to action and joyful with purpose.

But of course, it was all a farce, and of course, I'm alone again. And of course, when my father hears about this…and gets the bill for the second car I rented with his credit card number…he will continue to feel a spectacular lack of pride in his only son.

But I'm done. I've been mugged, and I've had my heart broken, and what do I have to show for it? Only the certainty that I am, in fact, nothing like my grandfather, and that I have, sadly, failed at the one thing that could have restored my family's faith in me.

This was a mistake. And I'm going home.

EPILOGUE: KADINJACA

I stand before *Kadinjaca,* looking up and shielding my eyes from the sun.

I did not go home.

Instead, I came here, where my grandfather lived and worked and married my grandmother, here where he was tortured. And here, apparently, where he was lucky to leave with his life. Here, where he and 400 other members of the Workers' Battalion held off 3,000 German soldiers for six hours. Here, where the sacrifice of nearly all of them gave civilians and party leadership time to escape.

I have read all the placards with historical information, and now I just stare at the statue, absentmindedly recognizing that my grandfather being a martyr makes him even one degree *more* impossible to emulate; recognizing that maybe emulation was never the point in the first place.

Kadinjaca looks like a starburst, or a bullet hole. It looks like Captain American punched his way through a towering slab of concrete to kill a Nazi. It stands in formation, carefully but inexplicably placed right in the middle of the green countryside, a Serbian Stonehenge.

Why did I stay?

Well…it might be hard to explain. I was there, at *Bratunak,* literally folding my clothes and typing the airport's coordinates into my GPS. I had decided to leave.

And then…I felt it.

It. It. I don't know what, but I felt it. A revelation, or a siren song, or the voice of someone else's God. I felt, suddenly, *something,* something that felt like nothing else, something that tore through the pain of a broken heart and the exhaustion of low self-esteem like a Eureka moment of pure insight. It felt like purpose.

It stopped me, caused me to drop heavily onto the front seat of the car, inspired me to dig through my backpack for my wallet and the scratched, worn family photo within.

My grandmother. Her son. His wife. Their child.

My parents, my grandparents, they all experienced something life-altering, the breakdown of all they knew to be normal, the uprooting of every aspect of their lives to come to America. I stared at that photo, and I thought about that, and I thought about our love. And then I understood, suddenly, that I was altered by their experiences, too. I was touched by my grandfather's torture, by the poverty of his childhood, by his final tour of the *Spomeniks,* a lap of triumph over the worst of man.

They say the genes of the grandchildren of Holocaust Survivors are literally changed by the trauma their grandparents endured, newborn DNA affected by physical suffering which occurred in the gene pool two whole generations ago. It's called epigenetics and, if trauma has the power to cause such evolutionary harm, then surely it must create some strength as well.

I was thinking these things in the shadow of *Bratunak,* and feeling purpose of some unknowable origin or direction, and it seemed, all of the sudden, less important to get to the airport than it had before. It seemed much more important, instead, to finish what I had started; to honor my grandfather, and to honor his sacrifices. It seemed much more important to experience what lies on the other side of this all.

I decided immediately to continue on to *Kadinjaca;* I didn't even stop to camp or treat myself to a cheap hostel. I drove through the night, propelled by possibility.

I don't have any idea, to be clear, what I am supposed to do now, now that I *haven't* given up, now that I've arrived at *Kadinjaca,* now that I am standing exactly where hundreds of ordinary men picked up arms to fight the Axis of Evil and, for a moment, actually made a difference.

I want to make a difference, too.

I want to be passionate. I want to discover what matters to me, what truly matters. I want, someday, a son to look at me the way my father must have looked at my grandfather, and I want to tell my son the story of where he came from. I want to tell him about the *Spomeniks.*

I stare at *Kadinjaca,* and I feel moved. I feel humbled. I feel like I have, finally, accomplished something, and I feel like maybe this could be the start of something brand new.

I do *not,* for the first time in forever, feel like I need to smoke pot.

About Shannon Frost Greenstein

Shannon Frost Greenstein resides in Philadelphia with her children, soulmate, and stubborn cats. She is the author of "Pray for

Us Sinners," a forthcoming fiction collection from Alien Buddha Press, and "More.", a poetry collection from Wild Pressed Books. Shannon is a Pushcart Prize and Best of the Net nominee, a Contributing Editor for Barren Magazine, and a former Ph.D. candidate in Continental Philosophy. Her work has appeared or is forthcoming in McSweeney's Internet Tendency, Pithead Chapel, X-R-A-Y Lit Mag, Cabinet of Heed, Ellipsis Zine, STORGY Mag, Lunate Fiction, Door Is a Jar, and elsewhere. Follow Shannon at shannonfrostgreenstein.com or on Twitter at @ShannonFrostGre. She comes up when you Google her.

Also by Shannon Frost Greenstein

More., Wild Pressed Books

http://www.wildpressedbooks.com/more1.html

Connect with Shannon Frost Greenstein

www.shannonfrostgreenstein.com

www.twitter.com/shannonfrostgre

www.instagram.com/zarathustra_speaks

www.facebook.com/shannongreenstein

2

The Halloween Blizzard: Two Hills and the Icy Plains of Doom

DAVID LANGE

Diary entry, October 28, 1991: "The mountain conditions are very questionable but I'm going to try to get across anyway—it's the prettiest route and by far my preferred routing. It'll be a tough drive."

My Instructor Upgrade Training Program was over. The Air Force gave me five days to get from Atwater, California back to my home base in Wichita, Kansas. I was going to try to make it home in three with a slight detour to visit my old college in Colorado Springs, Colorado. I knew friends who made the drive in two days. I'd heard of idiots who made it in one. My only company on this journey was my Chevy S-10 Blazer 4x4. Through three perilous days, a blizzard tracked eastward with me. I nearly died a half dozen times and I vowed, upon my return, that I would never own a vehicle without four-wheel drive—it saved my life, again and again.

I set out early on the morning of October 29th—my goal for day one was to conquer the Sierra Nevada Mountains and recover for the night into Salt Lake City, Utah. An older and wiser me would have elected to take the southern route home. At 25, I was more interested in reliving the breathtaking vistas that were etched in my brain following several spectacular trips across the mountains, especially a beautiful stretch of I-70 that wound its way through the Rocky Mountains. It was still fall and I gravely underestimated the brutality of the storm that was fast on my heels. In 1991, I had no cell phone to call for help or to check weather or road conditions up ahead. I navigated using my road atlas and, as necessary, my pocket compass. GPS units for automobiles were still years away.

A series of backroads took me north. The early morning drive was uneventful. As if fleeing before the tempest, the sun had long since disappeared from the daytime sky and an ominous darkness accompanied me as I made progress along some eerily desolate stretches of road. Where was everybody? Did they know something I did not? I intercepted I-80 somewhere north of Sacramento and felt a little more comfortable before detours took me, once again, across barren landscapes. Eventually, I reached the familiar foothills and began my ascent. The gentle snow flakes were hardly a portent of things to come. It wasn't long before the snows came in earnest. Between the fog and the blowing snow, visibility went down dramatically. I strained to see out ahead of me. Lane markings disappeared from view. My inclination was to reduce my speed significantly but I also knew that many trucks traveled these roads and I had no desire for an 18-wheeler to come barreling into me on a downhill stretch of interstate. If I couldn't see ahead, then neither could they. I was more confident in my ability to decelerate my small SUV than in a truck's ability to brake for me. So, I kept on at a moderate pace, just below the speed limit. While visibility was my primary concern, on this first leg of the trip, I did encounter a number of slick spots on those mountain roads which definitely got my attention. My entire body was tense as I wound my way through the mountains, four-wheel drive engaged. By the time darkness fell, I was exhausted. I popped some peppermint Lifesavers into my mouth to help revive me and they seemed to do the trick. Through the darkness and the mist, I was finally able to make out the distant lights of Salt Lake City. I made my way into town, my eyes stinging, and I hoped that there would be vacancies at the first hotel I found. Happily, there was. Little did I know that my winter driving experience had barely just begun.

Not wasting time for breakfast, I checked out of my hotel early in the morning and made a quick stop at a gas station to fill my tank. The degrading weather conditions filled me with a sense of urgency and I began to believe that every minute saved would help to keep me just ahead of the severe weather. My plan seemed to be working throughout the early hours of the morning. I tracked south along I-15 in order to reach I-70 where I would pick up my eastbound heading. Despite my concerns about the weather, I was still anxious to enjoy some mountain views along a familiar stretch of road. By the time I reached the Rockies, there was nothing to see. Again, the snows came and the lanes disappeared. My car fish-tailed, fighting for traction again and again, as I perilously passed a number of trucks, all creeping at a horse and buggy pace around the winding mountain roads. This was no longer a sightseeing pleasure drive; it had become a battle for survival. Ice was accumulating on my windshield wipers and the spray reservoir outlet nozzle quickly froze over. My wipers were doing the best they could to provide at least a limited amount of forward visibility; as much as was possible considering the blowing snow. I felt very uncomfortable but I continued my progress towards Denver. I can't overstate the sense of relief I felt as I began to slowly work my way back down the mountainous roads taking me into Denver. Denver, Colorado was reporting a record low temperature at five degrees Fahrenheit and, with the winds, the effective temperature was well into the negative range. Refueling my vehicle was pure misery. I was not equipped with a winter coat as I was not anticipating an October drive to turn into an Arctic expedition. As I held the icy-cold metal trigger on the gas pump, my hand nearly froze. The wind and blowing snow were tearing at my face. Could my eyeballs freeze? I wasn't sure. I squinted hard and tried to turn away from the direction of the wind. I considered my detour to Colorado Springs and quickly concluded that I had assumed enough risk for the day and could do without an icy rush hour detour two hours south of my primary route. The light was fading and, fortunately, I had enough sense not to let the temptation of a sentimental excursion cloud my judgment.

Retiring for the night in Denver, I went to bed with a false sense of security, having conquered two mountain ranges in less than ideal road conditions. I wasn't too worried about the long, straight, shot along I-70 into Kansas. That was plains country and there was little risk of sliding off a cliff. I'd sleep in a little bit longer just to give the plows a chance to clear the roads of the night's snow. I was sure my final day of driving would be the easiest and I was anticipating an afternoon recovery back at my apartment in Wichita.

I made no diary entry on October 31, 1991, Halloween. When I type the date into my computer's search engine, the first thing that pops up is "The Halloween Blizzard." A day later, my diary begins "We all can point to a day and say 'those were the worst driving conditions I ever saw'–October 31st, Halloween, was that day for me. I'm glad I lived through it and, if I thought roads might improve in the next few days, I might have called it quits—but I figured things would only get worse."

It was an incredibly frigid morning and the snow continued to fall heavily. Denver's temperature was the lowest recorded temperature ever for Halloween—a record only broken 28 years later, in 2019. This would be my third day of driving with no visible lane markers beneath the accumulated snow and ice. Visibility was awful and I kept telling myself that I'd break out into the clear sooner or later. I never did. I had no way of knowing that one of the most powerful "winter" storm systems in this nation's history was tracking right along with me and would be my traveling companion for the remainder of my journey. My car stayed in four-wheel drive mode the entire day as snow gradually transitioned into an even more dangerous freezing rain and sleet. The icy precipitation, layered upon the accumulated snow and slush, turned the entire interstate into a giant ice rink. My wiper blades worked furiously to maintain an aperture of sight, but even their heroic efforts could not fend off the impressive ice building up upon my windshield and upon the wipers themselves. My eyes desperately strained to see the road ahead. I noted in my diary that, if there had been any significant curves along the highway between Denver and Salina, Kansas, no one would have been able to keep to the road. As it was, an ever-increasing volume of vehicles lay motionless off to the sides of the interstate where they had slid into ditches, guard rails, or simply off into the shoulder. Smoke emanated from their tailpipes, indicating that the hapless travelers were burning their fuel to keep warm rather than to attempt any more forward progress on their journeys. The highway patrol was their last hope and the increasing number of flashing lights were proof that the first responders were out in force and attending as many stranded drivers as they could while others waited and hoped for rescue before their life-sustaining fuel ran out. Those who were able to maintain enough traction to stay on the road plodded along cautiously, knowing that their fate could just as easily be that of the unfortunate host of adventurers who succumbed to the brutal hand of Mother Nature.

As if things weren't bad enough, I encountered nearly unbearable road conditions between Hays and Salina, Kansas. It was the most dangerous stretch of road yet—something seemingly impossible to fathom considering the long, straight, stretch of flat earth separating the two cities. There were no places to stop and the freezing rain continued to pour down. Through some strange combination of snow, plowing, slush, more plowing, and then topped by freezing rain, the road had turned into a rutted and uneven surface that I can only equate to moguls on a ski slope. For one-hundred miles, over four hours, my car bounced and jumped as if I were driving over a series of continuous ice-covered speed bumps, one after the other. I had never experienced anything like that in my life. Even at 20 to 30 miles per hour, my car was bouncing and vibrating wildly and I had to fight to keep my vehicle on the road. The miles to Salina seemed infinite. My hands tightly gripped the steering wheel, my teeth were clenched, and my entire body was tense—it was absolutely exhausting. The darkness of the night only added to the dread. My hopes of a late afternoon return to Wichita had long-since faded. My new focus was on trying to keep myself alive, and sane, until Salina where I hoped I might find lodging for the night. My concern was that everyone else on the road was going to have the same idea. There aren't a lot of towns with hotels in that neck of the woods and I knew travelers would be scrambling for what rooms were available.

As I approached Salina, feeling like I had reached the limit of my endurance, I began to pick up my favorite Wichita radio station on my car radio. Less than 100 miles to go—maybe I can make it? The internal debate began. While I thought calling it quits right then and there was the safer option, I had serious doubts about finding lodging in Salina and it also seemed a shame to charge Uncle Sam for another night of hotel lodging when my own bed was a stone's throw away. As it turns out, it was going to be a really, really, really long stone's throw—I pushed on.

I was not on I-135 South for very long before I picked up on some burning flares in the road up ahead. With my windshield still heavily iced, I was struggling to assess the situation. I slowly followed the car ahead of me, not seeing any signs to indicate what I should be doing. The flares seemed randomly placed and absolutely confused me. Moments later, I saw the flashing lights of a police vehicle behind me. I pulled over. Expecting some helpful safety tips from the police officer who got out, I was instead rebuked for not turning off at the exit near the flares. "Yes, Sir; no, Sir; no excuse, Sir." I ran through all my basic military responses. I wanted to complain that the flares did nothing to advise drivers and that I had merely followed the path of the vehicle in front of me. Ultimately, I knew it was better just to take the heat and get on my way than to argue with a jerk who was probably having a pretty awful day, too. I didn't need any more stress in my day, although spending the night in a warm jail cell was seeming like a fairly decent option at that point. Apparently, I-135 was now closed. They should have closed I-70. I think they eventually did. Rather than turn me around, the highway patrol officer directed me to depart the interstate at the next available exit and I did just that. The detour only complicated my night's journey. As the entire interstate was shut down, I was going to have to somehow figure out how to get down to Wichita, Kansas using a series of backroads that were unfamiliar to me. Zigging this way, zagging that way, I worked my cardinal directions south and east until I saw the appropriate signage to get me back to Wichita. I breathed a huge sigh of relief as I finally entered the familiar city and, from there, memory took over and I cautiously made my way the remaining few miles towards my apartment. I was totally wiped out and the only thing I could think about was getting into my warm bed. And I was just about to do so when the phone rang. I must re-emphasize that I was not even supposed to be back home until Sunday night, November 3rd. I picked up the phone—it was my aircraft commander with one final Halloween night surprise for me. I was informed that I needed to come in the next morning (Friday) to plan a mission for a flight out to California on Monday and a week-long TDY (Temporary Duty) in California. The irony was not lost on me. I did my best to hold back the anger. I had just spent three days driving from California, in blizzard conditions, ne'er a lane marker to be seen, and nearly lost my life on several occasions, and *now* the Air Force wanted me to head right back?! Worse still, several other navigators were going to be on the flight, so I could have easily just met up with them in California as my services were not required to get the jet out to the West Coast. After a deep sigh, I told my aircraft commander that I'd be there. Phone receiver down, blankets pulled back, I was sound asleep within minutes.

I've been on countless road trips throughout the years. I've seen majestic mountains and beautiful stretches of southwestern dessert; I've experienced lovely views of the ocean and passed through many historic towns, occasionally stopping to visit sites of interest. But, if there's one journey that really stands out in my mind, it's the great Halloween nightmare drive in 1991. An older me looks back and questions my judgment—I certainly didn't choose the safest options and, in some ways, my decisions might make for some powerful talking points in a "what not to do" case study on winter driving safety. That aside, it was truly a memorable saga. That which does not kill us . . . often makes for a pretty decent story. Buckle up and drive safely!

About David Lange

Colonel David Lange was born and grew up on Long Island, New York. A graduate of the United States Air Force Academy, he served for 30 years as an Active Duty officer in the United States Air Force before retiring in 2018. Colonel Lange is a decorated combat veteran, and flew numerous combat, combat support, and humanitarian relief missions during his career. He was awarded the prestigious Institute of Navigation Superior Achievement Award in recognition of his life-long accomplishments as a practicing navigator. David loves sharing stories of hope and inspiration and, in 2020, he published his memoir, *Quest: My Journey Through La Mancha.*

Also by David Lange

Quest: My Journey Through La Mancha

Connect with David Lange

https://www.davidlangequest.com

3

Someday We'll Laugh About This

WILLIAM JOHN ROSTRON

On July 11, 1989, we almost died. It was an *almost* tragedy that will remain in my waking thoughts forever. However, the takeaway here, of this true story, is that not only did we survive, but that the subsequent events proved to be humorous—so much so that we continuously found ourselves using the phrase, "Someday we'll laugh about this."

Our family of five had just started home from a fun-filled two-week stay in Disney World. We could stay for such an extended period because costs were significantly lower when you stayed in Disney's campground, and you brought a travel trailer with you from New York. However, all good things must end, and we began our long trek home.

I had driven most of the day and night from Orlando to the South Carolina border when my wife Marilyn took over the driving. I joined my sons Justin (14) and Jarrod (12) in the king-size bed that I had made when I customized our Dodge van. My daughter Brittany (6) had decided to co-pilot with mommy in the front. However, shortly after being tucked in her seat belt, she joined the rest of us in slumber. Because of this, my wife was the only one awake when an eighteen-wheeler side-swiped our trailer and sent us jack-knifing across I-95.

As the trailer slid into the inner curb of the road, it crashed on its side and whipped the van across the grass median as such a speed that the vehicle turned over six times before it came to rest as a twisted wreck. In a dazed horror, I realized a few facts. The two inches of foam that I had installed in the walls for the "plush-look" had had a cushioning effect that protected my sons and me during the crash's trauma. The engineering needed to put in a sunroof had kept the top of the van from totally collapsing on my wife's head – it had stopped only inches away. My third realization was the most terrifying. I found myself upside down in the front passenger seat. That seat had been occupied by my daughter, who was no longer in the van. A severed seat belt lay inches from my eyes, and the breeze that blew on my face told me that the front windshield was no longer there. That very moment, thirty years later, still wakes me in the middle of the night in cold sweats and haunts me with what could have been. However, I did promise that this was an *almost* tragedy with lighter moments to follow.

Within minutes, my son Justin kicked opened the crumbled rear doors, and the three of us exited in search of six-year-old Brittany. It seemed like an eternity until I spotted her sitting in a mud puddle inches away from the road we had left behind. She saw me and started to walk toward me, and I ran to her, all the while searching for injuries that were not there. As the boys ran to tell their mother that their sister was safe, I looked at the miracle of my unscathed daughter and asked her what had happened?

"I don't know, Daddy. I was sleeping, and when I woke up, the van was rolling away. Where did you guys go? Did I miss anything?" The comedy had begun.

When the state police arrived minutes later, they rapidly did three things. They extricated my wife from her trapped position, put her in a neck brace and on a stretcher, and then proceeded to give her a ticket! I hid my rage as I asked why the state trooper was giving her the citation.

"Dangerous driving caused the crash." When I got over my disbelief, I explained that a trucker, who was now long gone, had hit us. I also explained that I knew for a fact our van was incapable of hitting speeds over 55 while towing our 22-ft trailer. In a scene reminiscent of the movie, *My Cousin Vinny*, he answered, "You're in the boonies, sir. If you don't like it, go back up North." I almost lost it before realizing that this officer would determine the next few hours of my family's existence.

As we all took off in the ambulance, I watched every one of our possessions head in the complete opposite direction. When I asked about this, the same trooper explained that the van, the trailer, and all our remaining belongings were headed thirty miles north to the AAA location, and we would head 30 miles south to the hospital. "That's the way it is," he said, and I said under my breath, "Yeah, I know, I'm in the boonies, sir."

We arrived at the hospital and were told to wait for the doctor. OK, so I think that he's with another patient until the hospital administrator says, "Yeah, he doesn't live too far away." In this unreal experience, I should have learned not to question anybody, but I had to ask her politely why there was not a doctor *in* the hospital.

"Do doctors in hospitals in New York just sit around and wait for patients to come in?" She didn't mention *being in the boonies,* so I did *not* say, "Well, Yeah!" When the doctor finally arrived, each member of my family took turns seeing him. By the time it was my turn, my knee and ankle were beginning to swell. I was directed to an X-ray machine as a "technician" entered the room. I knew that she seemed a bit young and could not have studied anything beyond freshmen English. This observation was confirmed when she could not find the on/off switch for the machine. When the doctor looked in the room and reminded her to "line up the scotch tapes sections over his injured knee," I knew that we were in trouble. When I advised her that my ankle also needed to be looked at, she responded in her sweetest Southern voice, "No problem, darling, I'll just raise this machine a little higher and get a picture of both." I was about to tell her that I didn't think that was how it should be done when I gave up and realized that we would all get real checkups when we got home. And then the real fun began.

I took stock of my family. No one was bleeding and, though my wife wore a neck brace, our only visible injuries were black and blue marks on everyone except miracle child Brittany. Like I said, this was an *almost* tragedy. Yet my observation also showed that we were covered in milk from a cooler, had torn clothing, and I had no shoes. We were also sixty miles away from our possessions. I approached the hospital administrator with my dilemma.

"Where can I rent a car?"

"We're a small town. We don't have a car rental."

"Where can we catch a train?"

"It doesn't run through here."

"A bus?"

"Nope."

Frustrated, I asked if she had any suggestions about how I could travel the distance to our belongings. In a million years, I could never have foreseen the next words out of her mouth, but I will always remember them.

"Of what religious persuasion are you all? Perhaps someone of similar persuasion will help you in your time of need." Was this a loaded question, I wondered. I knew that I was deeply entrenched in the Southern bible belt, and here we were New York Italian Catholics. I had taught my children that honesty is the best policy. Besides that, twenty centuries of martyrs had gained sainthood by not denying their religion. I boldly answered, "Catholic." In the thirty years of telling this story, no one has ever guessed her excited reply.

"I know THE Catholic who lives in this county. I went to high school with her. I will see if she will help you because of your shared beliefs." She truly spoke like that. I had mixed feelings about there being a solution to my problem and the use of the word "THE" limiting my chances. An hour later, the door swung open, and the administrator announced quite weirdly, "THE Catholic is here." Two thoughts immediately crossed my mind. 1) Doesn't she know this woman's name? 2) She was incorrect because the woman had brought her father, who was also Catholic–so there were two! Yet, we finally saw a road home. And still, the story wasn't over for the Rostron family or that tiny little hospital.

As we were about to begin our sixty-mile trek with "THE Catholics," a woman frantically ran to the hospital doors holding an unconscious baby in her arms. As she ran to the doctor, I only heard the words "not breathing." Through closed doors, I listened to the desperate machinations of the doctor's rescue attempt, followed by the wailing of the baby's cry. It quickly occurred to me that the doctor had only been at the hospital because *we* had arrived. Had our *almost* tragedy saved a life? We would all be going home, and so would that baby.

The trek north started awkwardly with a strange silence that began when we mentioned our family name. Finally, the father spoke, "Are you really Catholic?" I guess my English protestant name made him think that we were perhaps northern con-artists who were faking our religion to travel on his dime. I quickly had to explain the Romeo and Juliet story of my parents. My father's New England WASP family shunned him for marrying an Italian Catholic. He then had the nerve to convert. I also explained that my wife Marilyn was a full-blooded third-generation Italian despite her very un-Italian first name. Secure in the thought that we had not hoodwinked them, we continued on our journey. Most of our friends were amazed that we bonded with the only Catholics in the county, and that had enabled us to begin our journey home. However, a Jewish friend was not amused. His only comment was, "You do realize that *I* would still be there!"

As the conversation and the journey continued, I asked how they could practice their religion if, indeed, they were the only Catholics in the county. The answer was one for the books. They had bonded with the dozen or so Catholics from the five surrounding counties, and when possible, a mass was held.

"So, I guess that you can't always get a priest for such a small group?" I asked.

"No, the priest comes from Charleston whenever we ask. It's our "church" that is not always available for us." Now I was confused.

"A local funeral home generously volunteers to give us a room to use. . . if no one has died that week. So, we all check the obituaries to see if there will be a mass that Sunday. It gives us a second reason to pray for the health of our neighbors and friends."

Later, I mentioned that both my wife and I were public school teachers. Ann, "THE Catholic," smiled and told us so was she. After we answered her questions about education and general teaching conditions in the North, we asked about the public schools where she taught. She replied rather matter-of-factly that they were "not so good." I pushed her further to explain.

"Well, last week, a matter came before the school board that we found disturbing. Our elementary school principal had a problem because the floor in one classroom had rotted, and there was a two-foot in diameter hole. The board president asked which side of the room the hole was located. When principal said the left, he answered by saying, 'Tell the students to stay on the right side of the room then.'"

"But don't they care about their own kids' safety?" I asked.

"That's just it," Ann said, "Their kids don't go to the schools. All the white kids go to private or religious schools that aren't integrated. It's their way around the Supreme Court ruling.

"So, there are no white kids in the schools?"

"No, my kids are there, as well as most of the other teachers."

"So, you took a stand."

"Well, it's easy to take a stand when you don't have a choice. Because the board and the voters don't care about attracting and keeping great teachers, our pay is so low that we can't afford the private schools that their children attend."

I know that three decades have passed since that moment and that the reality she was describing to me has changed. However, I was never prouder of the fact that my wife and I had chosen to raise our children in a diverse school district.

When we arrived at our destination, we said goodbye to Ann, THE Catholic and Fred, her father (and other Catholic). We expressed our gratitude and told them that we would pray for their neighbors' health and safety so that they could go to mass that Sunday. We shared a good laugh. Then we saw the remains of our van and trailer and stopped laughing.

There were no words to describe the crumbled wreck of the vehicle we had all been riding. We stood silently, trying to comprehend the incredible nature of our survival. We had escaped with our lives, but fate had not been so kind to our van and trailer. We decided that we would scavenge what possessions we could, rent a van, and find our way home.

The AAA agent met us by the ruins of our possessions and invited us into his office to explain what they had salvaged and what AAA could do for us. He was efficient in a down-home way, and, after about an hour, Chet Smith, AAA representative, had completed his business with us and asked if we had any other questions.

"I have Allstate insurance. Do you know how I can get in contact with the claims department?" He pointed across the hall to a door that said Allstate Sales and Claims. Just when I was beginning to think how convenient this was, in walked the agent, *Chet Smith, Allstate Representative*. With a straight face, he sat down at the desk, and unbelievably said, "How can I help you folks?" I could not decide if Chet Smith, AAA rep, was being funny or if he had a stupid twin brother who also used the same name. We put in our claim, and not surprisingly, he knew what damage the van and trailer had suffered and how much we would get paid. He had the advantages of being the same company that towed our possessions and, therefore, had been looking at them for the last day.

"Any questions?" he asked when we completed our business behind door number two.

"Where can I rent a car to get home?" I asked.

"In the office next door," he answered. We got up and walked to our right. We sat for a few minutes waiting before *Chet Smith, Hertz rental agent,* sat down in front of us. My wife looked in disbelief, and I said sarcastically, "Nice to meet you . . . again." I was beginning to think I was in a Monty Python sketch. But I played along with the farce.

"I'd like to rent a car one way to New York."

"THE car is out right now," was his answer. I don't know what amazed me more: Chet Smith in his third office/third employment situation, or the fact that the car rental service only possessed one car? I also questioned the seemingly local dependence on the word "THE."

"Let me guess. If I ask you if you have a van to rent, you will tell me that "THE van" is out."

"Well, yeah," he said with a sheepish look on his face. However, he quickly added that he could borrow one from Charleston; it would just take extra time and money. Did we have a choice? After that, I mentioned that we would need transportation to get to a motel that was five miles away. (no bus–no taxi–we asked)

"Well, I have an old school bus that you can rent for the day." Having our first positive response to any transportation request in two days, I quickly said yes. One of my wise-ass sons chimed in, "A school bus, really? Don't you know it's summer and we're on vacation?"

"Here are the directions. You can walk. See ya there," I wasn't in the mood to give father-of-the-year answers at that point.

I then asked Chet Smith (AAA rep, Allstate agent, and Hertz rental manager) to borrow the phone to find out if there were any vacancies at the motel. I saw him rise from his seat and swore we were going to enter door number four for *Chet Smith, travel agent.* When I mentioned this to him, he told me I was being silly. He was just going to get his cousin Johnny's phone number. He owned the motel. So, we got on our school bus and drove to Johnny Smith's motel.

The motel provided very seriously needed showers and a place to change into fresh clothes—and I finally had shoes! However, my mind was spinning, and I didn't sleep much. I had determined that the sooner we got home, the sooner we could get real medical exams with actual X-rays. We salvaged anything of worth from the trailer and lined the bare van with every cushion that we could fit from the trailer's beds. I decided that somehow, I would drive the 900 miles home without stopping. Wrong!

By the time I had reached the Jersey Turnpike, I had realized that I was so seriously exhausted that I was putting my family's lives in danger. As they slept, I barely was able to pull into the first rest stop. With 48 hours of exhaustion closing in, I pulled into a parking spot facing the side of a building and fell asleep right where I sat. This choice would lead to the second scariest moment of the whole ordeal.

Three hours later, I awoke dazed and confused, not even comprehending where I was. As I opened my eyes, I was disoriented. All that I knew was that I was sitting in the driver's seat with my hands clutching the steering wheel and my foot on the brake–and a brick wall was looming only a few feet in front. My sleep-deprived state of consciousness did not register that I was not in a *moving* vehicle. My impending (and imaginary) destruction was imminent. I let out a blood-curdling scream that awoke the four other members of the family.

"What's happening?" responded my now panicking wife. However, by then, I was aware of what was going on.

"Nothing, a bad dream," I answered.

"Not true, what happened?" she demanded, and I told her the truth. For the first time since the crash, I heard the sound of giggling in the back.

"It's not that funny," I protested, and my son Jarrod whispered to the others.

"He screamed louder than Mom when she *actually had the accident*!"

More giggling. And I loved the sound of it.

I have written quite a bit in the ensuing years, including three novels, but I have never been able to put this story down on paper until now. Perhaps, there is a statute of limitations on bad memories. Or maybe thirty years of good memories have exorcised the terror of the thirty seconds of not knowing what had happened to our lost little girl. With marriages and births, our band of five has blossomed into an even dozen. We are always together and having a good time. There are plenty of shared experiences that we enjoy passing on to the children's spouses and our grandchildren. But we never talk about a certain early morning in South Carolina. Maybe that will change.

One final event occurred in our incredulous misadventure. I now look back at the final scene with an ironic eye. As we pulled up to our home, exhausted both physically and mentally, we only thought of pulling onto our property, grabbing a few items, and finding our way to *our* beds in *our* home. But somebody up there has a twisted sense of humor.

The extremely rare occurrence of a mini-tornado on Long Island had downed a tree from our front lawn and left it across our driveway. Before anyone could even ask what we were going to do, I just parked in the street, turned the engine off, and said, "Tomorrow's another day." As I exited the van, I took nothing with me besides my sleeping daughter in my arms. I maneuvered over the fallen locust tree and waited by the front door for the others.

In 2011, I would vividly remember those last moments of our *almost* tragic, yet insanely comedic trip home. While at our daughter's wedding, I watched as my two tuxedoed sons walked arm in arm with their mother to her seat. I could not help but flashback to that moment twenty-two years ago when they supported my wife's bruised body as three of them climbed over the tree in roughly the same configuration that they then appeared in the church. Only moments later, I walked my daughter down the aisle to "give her away" to the man she loved, yet for a few seconds, I was back on that driveway, on *that* morning, and at our journey's end. As I gazed at her in her gown, I thought, *this* almost didn't happen.

However, on that July morning in 1989, I could not know the future. I could not know of all the good times that were ahead. I could not foresee all the holiday gatherings, the graduations, the family jokes, and long-standing traditions—all those bonding moments that eternally cemented our family ties. I could not know of the grandchildren that would come into our lives. On that morning, three decades ago, I only knew that we were all alive and that *we would have a future*. And I remember thinking to myself how fortunate we had been. Or was it blessed?

I mumbled, and the then six-year-old Brittany stirred in my arms.

"What did you say, Daddy?"

"My little miracle, someday we're going to laugh about this."

About William John Rostron

Born and raised in Queens, NY, William John Rostron now splits his time between his home on Long Island and traveling the country in his Tiffin motorhome. When not writing, he is busy completing a bucket list of travel adventures. In the past 16 years, he and his wife Marilyn have traveled 120,000 miles. These journeys have taken them to the 48 contiguous states, 133 national parks, all 30 major league baseball stadiums, 154 cities and towns, two Canadian provinces, and a variety of unusual experiences and locations.

He recently completed a trilogy of novels steeped in the music and culture of the late 20th and early 21st centuries. *Band in the Wind, Sound of Redemption,* and *Brotherhood of Forever* have received critical acclaim from Writers Digest, the Online Book Club Review, as well as many other reviewers.

In the past, he has published over two dozen non-fiction articles in newspapers and magazines. These writings included four full-page op-eds in New York Newsday. He was also presented an award by Nelson DeMille for his historical fiction short story, "The Last Artifact."

Three of his short pieces were accepted into the Visible Ink Anthology in 2018, 2019, and 2020 Each year, a dozen works are chosen for reading and presentation on stage in New York City. In 2018, "Pretty Flamingo" was given this honor. As an encore, "In the Garden of Eden" was performed in 2019. Both of these are available for viewing on www.williamjohnrostron.com or on YouTube by using "Visible Ink" plus each title. In 2020, his short work "Ava's Bubble" was read by Tony and Emmy nominee, Victor Garber on a nationally televised streaming show.

In his previous career, the author instructed students from the ages of 9 to 90. Throughout his life, he taught elementary school, middle school, high school, college, adult education, and teacher training. He holds degrees from Queens College, Stony Brook University, and Long Island University.

Also by William John Rostron

Novels:

Band in the Wind

Sound of Redemption

Brotherhood of Forever

Recent Short Pieces: "Pretty Flamingo", "In the Garden of Eden", "Ava's Bubble", "When the Music's Over."

Connect with William John Rostron

www.WilliamJohn Rostron.com

PART IV

I Can't Find My Flashlight

It was a cold, dark night and the young boy's flashlight was nowhere to be found. The camping trip had been everything he had hoped for; that is, until the sun had set, stranding him in the unfamiliar woods that he had hoped would be the setting of his next great summer adventure. With no light, no parents, and no way to call for help, all the boy could do was wait out the night and hope that his nightmares would not claim him as their next victim.

Sound familiar? The tradition of storytelling is one that has taken on many forms, one of the most notable being that of the campfire horror story. In this Halloween inspired edition of The Red Penguin Collection, prepare to be amazed by the diverse range of entries our authors have written and the tremendous worlds they have created. From the spectacular to the spooktastic, the stories you are about to read are not for the faint of heart.

1

DIE XIAN (Ouija Board)

FRANCES LU-PAI IPPOLITO

I want to tell you first that this story is based on true events. The point is not to scare you, but if something should happen to me, I wanted someone, anyone, to know.

Decades later, I remember that autumn afternoon in 1989, two weeks before my twelfth birthday. At 3pm, two of my aunts, my mother, and Popo (my grandmother) sat at separate sides of a square wooden dining table covered by a layer of Plexiglas laying over a coarse red tablecloth. The metal condiment caddy that held pickled peppers and egg roll plum sauce had been cast aside and was tilted awkwardly against the backrest of a spare chair. The caddy kept company with four sets of napkins, utensils, and Chinese Zodiac paper placemats that the women had taken off the table to make space for one of my yellow sheets of construction paper.

Typically, during the break between lunch and dinner service, my family closed the Moon Gate Inn Restaurant. That day was different. My recently married Aunt Joyce was visiting and she had insisted that they pass the time with some fun as a family – a game.

I stood in the gap between Popo's and Aunt Joyce's chairs, watching them sip tea and write Chinese characters onto the sheet of paper. Glancing down, I couldn't read most of the characters scrawled across the paper, but I recognized the word for "no," "yes," and "love." One Chinese character, the one for "home," was printed larger than the rest and held the spot in the center of a red circle drawn in the middle of the page. In that circle, Aunt Xiao-Lin, placed a quarter, head side up.

"Is this a good idea?" Aunt Xiao-Lin asked the others.

"It's just a game," Aunt Joyce said, using her teeth to tear into the plastic wrapper of a fortune cookie that she'd picked out from the restaurant's endless store. "Maybe it'll help you get a husband finally." She smirked and offered Aunt Xiao-Lin an unwrapped cookie.

The only unmarried adult woman in the family, Aunt Xiao-Lin rolled her eyes and stuck out her tongue, but she took the cookie and broke the crisp shell in half. She popped a piece into her mouth and crunched without bothering to read the slip of paper inside. My mother laughed and Popo shook her head with a smile. It must have been nice for them to have this moment of banter with each other. My Aunt Joyce had moved to Florida five months ago with her new American husband and this was the first reunion for the sisters.

"Ruyi, please throw these away for me?" Aunt Xiao-Lin said, handing me the spent wrappers and paper. I nodded, but stuffed everything into my back pocket with the gum wrapper and other garbage I'd cached there until the pocket got too full.

I felt my mother's eyes on me and saw that she was watching with disapproval, but she said nothing. Instead, she seemed eager to keep the gathering peaceful and light.

"Shall we begin?" She asked the others. They nodded and smiled, and I recall vividly seeing but not understanding the bright excitement in their eyes.

Noticing me hovering by the table, my mother tried to shoo me away. "Ruyi, go play somewhere else."

"But I want to see what you're doing. Is it like Mah-Jong? I know how to play that," I whined. There were no other children and I wanted so badly to be included with the adults.

"You're too young for this," she answered.

"It's ok," Aunt Xiao-Lin said quickly, grinning at me. "Stand by me."

At twenty-eight, she was the youngest of my aunts and my favorite – the fun one who played pretend and gave me candy. I hopped over to her side of the table and quietly watched as each woman placed a single fingertip on the edge of the quarter and began to chant, "Spirit, Spirit, please come out."

A minute or two passed, but nothing happened while their fingers remained pressed to the quarter. They chanted again. Bored, I wandered away to a nearby booth of cold burgundy leather to pour driblets of soy sauce out of the glass dispenser into clean tea cups. There, I split a pair of bamboo chopsticks and used the tips to swirl the black liquid in the bottom of the tea cups.

But my attention shifted again to the adults when they gasped and their arms lurched in disjointed movements back and forth along the table. It was like seeing the washing machine work with the lid up where the clothes were being dragged along by the twisting and turning of agitators, except these clothes still had people in them. Confused, I ran behind Aunt Xiao-Lin's chair and peered over her shoulder at the four fingertips crowded together on top of the quarter. For several revolutions, the quarter continued to slide in halting spirals around the paper, taking the fingers of my family's women with it.The quarter abruptly stopped in front of Aunt Xiao-Lin. Standing this close to my aunt, I could not help thinking that she was so pretty with delicate, pale skin and long silky black hair. I wanted to look like her when I grew up.

"Alright, who's pushing it? This position is making my back sore," my mother complained through pinched breath. Her seat was farthest from Aunt Xiao-Lin, which forced her to lean across to maintain the contact between the coin and her fingertip.

"The ghost is here! Now we can ask questions!" Aunt Joyce said, her head wagged up and down gleefully.

A real ghost? I thought and a chill ran down my spine. Was she joking?

"Ask a question," my mother instructed Aunt Xiao-Lin.

She hesitated a moment before speaking. "Umm, are you a ghost?"

The quarter skated across the paper, roaming to the edges and corners before gliding back to sit over a character. Yes.

"Did you die here?" My mother asked.

Yes.

"I'm scared," Aunt Xiao-Lin murmured. She seemed paler than just a few moments before.

With her free hand, my mother placed her index finger over her own lips to hush my aunt.

"Man or woman?" Popo asked next. The quarter circled again and the room was silent except for the "shooshing" noise of metal running over the surface of paper fibers.

"Nan," Popo said. A man.

"Will my sister get married soon?" Aunt Joyce grinned at Aunt Xiao-Lin.

"Seriously?" Aunt Xiao-Lin frowned.

The quarter moved to "Yes."

"See, I'm helping you," Aunt Joyce said to Aunt Xiao-Lin, winking. "When?"

The quarter passed and stopped over two characters. Tonight.

Aunt Xiao-Lin scowled. "That's not funny, Joyce."

"I'm not moving it."

"Yes, you are!"

"How old are you?" My mother asked, probably trying to ease the tension.

The quarter passed over the written numbers, 1 through 100, before stopping on 35.

"So young," Popo remarked with what seemed like pity, smoothing the raven cropped curls on her head with her free hand. I recognized this gesture. Popo did this at the line in the DMV or grocery store when she took me to translate her requests into English. She was nervous.

"Did you have a wife or children?" Aunt Xiao-Lin asked this time.

No.

Aunt Joyce, always so fearless, asked, "How did you die?"

Murder.

"This is not good," Popo said uneasily, "a vengeful spirit. We should ask him to leave."

Though there was no question, the quarter moved to cover the word "No."

My Popo's face instantly bleached of color and she ran her hand roughly through her hair again. "No more game. We need to stop," she said.

Again, the quarter moved without a question, circling before returning to "No."

Aunt Xiao-Lin squirmed uneasily in her chair and her arm sagged.

"Keep your finger on!" Aunt Joyce hissed. "Bad luck to take it off before the Spirit leaves." Aunt Xiao-Lin bowed her head and nodded. But her eyes looked away from the paper, down at the floor.

"Are you the only ghost in this restaurant?" Aunt Joyce asked, redirecting her gaze to the paper.

No.

"How many?"

I craned my neck over my Aunt's shoulder so I could see what number it would pick. Instead of a numeral, the coin stopped on the character "duo" for a lot.

"Why?" My mother asked reflexively.

It answered: fire, murder.

"See!" Aunt Joyce said eagerly. "A-Mei was right. Something bad did happen here." However, from the tense and blank faces of the others, no one else seemed pleased by this confirmation.

A-Mei was Aunt Joyce's friend from Tampa, Florida who came two days ago to visit. She was in her fifties and sported a small beehive hairdo that was paired with blue eyeshadow and a chili red lipstick. As a young woman in Taiwan, A-Mei married an American military man and had lived in this country for far longer than any of us. She was nice enough, but struck me as odd when she refused to walk through the restaurant she had driven hours to see. There is something down there, she told us in the kitchen while pointing at the door to the basement. "I can't stay here," she said and immediately got in her car to drive back home.

"Let's stop. This isn't fun anymore," Aunt Xiao-Lin said in a strained whisper.

The quarter moved again. No.

"We are sorry for your deaths. We will burn paper money to help bring you peace," Popo's voice came out louder than usual, forced through her tight, pursed lips. I knew she meant paper offerings in the form of money, houses, clothes, food, and other things that, once burned, were believed to turn into usable things for spirits in the afterlife.

The quarter moved. Yes.

Popo nodded in relief. "Thank you Spirit for your kindness and compassion. We ask now for you to return home to rest." But instead of traveling back to the center of the paper marked as "home," the coin moved to two words in succession, "bu-yao." Don't want to.

Popo's smile changed immediately into a flat thin line. "Do you have another request?"

Yes.

Popo spoke slowly, like she was carefully choosing and measuring out each word – afraid to bargain, "We may not be able to help you. But we can, at least, hear your request."

The coin circled again to pass over several words, forming the sentence, "I like her." It then stopped in a blank space in front of Aunt Xiao-Lin.

"Joyce, that's enough." Aunt Xiao-Lin asked, her face ashen and her shoulders shaking.

But both Aunt Joyce's eyes and mouth were wide open. "I swear, I'm not doing anything. I'm not moving it."

"Then, you," Aunt Xiao-Lin gave my mother a hurt look.

My mother shook her head. My mother, the serious one, was the last person who would purposefully move the coin as a prank. And, of course, no one would accuse Popo of frightening Aunt Xiao-Lin this way.

Popo's face hardened. "Spirit, you are wise and must know that the living cannot be with the dead."

The quarter moved to "No," and then immediately returned to its place in front of my aunt.

"It wants a ghost bride," Aunt Xiao-Lin whispered.

The quarter moved twice. Yes. Mine.

"You can't have her. She will not marry the dead." Popo said angrily. As she said this, I felt the temperature in the room drop until goosebumps covered my arms and neck, prickling against the fabric of my long-sleeved turtleneck.

The quarter moved to several characters. If not her, then the other unmarried girl.

"She's a child!" My mother shouted.

I felt my heart seize. "Are . . . are you talking about me?" I stuttered out loud.

The quarter answered me three times, the same way. Mine. Mine. Mine.

At that, Aunt Joyce jumped up, lifted her finger off the quarter, and pulled the sheet of paper out from under the other women.

"Joyce, you said–" Aunt Xiao-Lin began.

Aunt Joyce interrupted her while ripping the paper into several pieces. "I know what I said, but it's just a game. We'll burn a lot of joss paper for the dead, everyday for a whole month. It'll be fine." But I noticed above us that the red silk lanterns hanging from the ceiling had started swaying although there was no wind inside our building.

As if a switch had been flipped, the adults scrambled to toss out the torn pieces of paper and the quarter was dropped into a "Feed the Children" donation box sitting by the cash register. Almost by conspiracy, the adults refused to talk about the die xian board.

"Mommy, what happened? What's a ghost bride?" I asked her as she tied an oil splotched black apron around her waist.

"Don't meddle in things you don't understand. Go into the office. We have work to do." My mother nudged me towards the office at the back of the kitchen and shut the door after scooting me inside.

At about 11pm that night, we stood by the red lacquered double doors at the restaurant entrance. It was a moment of goodbye and we lingered, memorizing each other in the penumbra of shadows and lights created by the streaking headlamps of a passing car and the single signal light hanging low at the intersection next to the restaurant.

"Give Aunty Joyce a hug. She's leaving early tomorrow morning with Popo," my mother said to me.

"Oh, my big girl. Be good and listen to your mom." Aunt Joyce squeezed me tight. I hugged her back. She was fierce and scared me at times, but I admired her boldness.

"Drive safe," Aunt Xiao-Lin hugged her next.

"I will. Zaijian le!" Aunt Joyce got into her car where Popo was already waiting. We continued to wave at them until she drove away.

"Can I stay with you tonight?" I begged Aunt Xiao-Lin, holding onto her right hand with both of mine. Aunt Xiao-Lin always let me dress up in her clothes and try on make-up.

"Ruyi, it's too late. Next time," my mother said.

"It's ok, she can stay over tonight. We'll make pancakes for breakfast." My aunt patted my head.

"Please Mom! Please, please!"

Are you sure?" My mom asked my aunt.

"Yes, I'd appreciate the company," she said, stroking my bobbed hair with her gentle fingers.

"Ok, see you tomorrow morning. And, Ruyi, be good and listen to your aunt." She kissed my head and we walked to the parking lot together. My mother left first as Aunt Xiao-Lin and I climbed into her Pontiac hatchback. She buckled me into the passenger seat and my head rolled onto the window. I was tired and ready to fall asleep in the car.

"That's strange," My aunt said and I opened my eyes when she turned on the overhead car light. She dug into her unzipped pink purse, pulling out her checkbook, eyeglass holder, and a stick of fresh gum.

"What's wrong, Aunty?"

"I must have left the apartment keys inside. I only have the car and restaurant keys with me." She held two sets of keys in the palm of her hand and she examined them one by one in the weak lighting. She sighed, "I'll have to go back inside to find them."

"Oohh . . . aaw. . . kay," I yawned and began unbuckling myself. She placed her hand over mine.

"You stay here. Lock the doors and don't go outside. I'll just be a couple of minutes."

I nodded and reclined my backrest. Aunt Xiao-Lin opened the car door and checked that each one was locked before turning off the overhead light and closing the driver's side door. With only the signal light at the intersection to illuminate the night, I watched the darkness swallow her bit by bit as she strode back towards the restaurant doors. Though I was sleepy then, I remember clearly now, that as she reached the doors, I saw a dim light flash across one of the windows on the opposite side of where she was standing. It was there only for a moment and I dismissed it, at the time, as the reflection of headlights on the glass.

About thirty minutes later, I was startled awake by a loud scream. As my eyes focused, I immediately scanned the parking lot in the direction of where I thought the scream came from. This late at night, the streets were completely empty without a single car in any direction. The gas station and convenience store across the street were closed. My heart started to race as I realized that I was completely alone in the only car parked in the restaurant lot. No one else knew we were here.

Staring at the restaurant and questioning whether I should leave the car to check on my aunt, I saw the lights flicker on and then off through the restaurant windows. I thought she must have tried to turn the lights on, but got hurt or fell in the dark.

Still, the idea of walking alone into an unlit building was unsettling and, with armpits slick with cold sweat, I struggled to lift the latch of the car lock with quivering fingers. A brisk wind slammed against my face when I finally opened the door. I wrapped my arms around myself and tucked my chin as I sprinted through the piercing gale to the restaurant entrance. As soon as I touched the doorknob, the unlocked door swung wide open and I rushed into the foyer to escape the biting wind.

Unaccustomed to navigating the space in the dark, my hands were outstretched in front of me, groping the space ahead as I stepped carefully towards where I thought the order counter would be. If I could reach the control box there, I would be able to turn on the lights in the main dining room. But when I stepped forward, I heard a noise from my right – a soft panting coming from the deep recesses of the room. It was too dark for me to see beyond the silhouettes of chairs stacked on top of tables, but the room felt occupied by another presence, something alive and breathing. Maybe even watching me. The hairs on my neck bristled and I trembled as a gust of wind pushed the door open again.

"Aunty? Is that you?" I whispered, my voice breaking slightly. There was no answer, except for the whining of the hinges from the doors rocking in the wind.

I took a breath and forced myself to continue walking in the direction of the counter. When my fingers finally met the ledge, I grabbed it like the wall of a pool, clinging as if the solid firmity could protect me from the suffocating dark. Quickly, I slipped behind the counter and opened the top drawer, feeling for the dials, slides, and switches of the control panel which controlled most of the lights in the main dining room. Unable to read any of the labels, I flipped on all the switches with the meaty part of my hand. Instantly, light from the chandeliers flooded the room and the music from "I saw him standing there," by Tiffany blasted at maximum volume. To stop the ache in my head, my hands flew down to turn off the radio and lessen the brightness.

The room was almost the same as how we left it hours ago. On all but one table, the chairs were stacked on top, leaving the carpet clear. However, unlike the rest, the circular banquet table in the back corner had all eight chairs neatly placed around it. By design, even under normal conditions, this table was different. It sat on a raised platform that elevated it above the others on lower ground. Used for celebrations, like weddings, the platform placed the bride and groom on display before their guests. I knew that my mother could have easily forgotten to put the chairs up; it had been a busy day. My mother, however, would not have left plates of food on the lazy susan.

Feeling braver under the bright lights and in the familiar room, I skirted past the rows of tables and clambered up the platform. The banquet table was set for two – a pair of plates, rice bowls, soup spoons, chopsticks, and teacups. A teapot and large platters of raw foods weighed down the lazy susan, making it slow and sluggish when I attempted to rotate it. As it circled, I made a mental count of the bleeding ball of ground meat, a whole unscaled fish, a raw chicken with the head and feet intact, and twitching lobsters and crabs taken live from the tanks. A child of the kitchen, the uncooked food itself was not frightening and did not disturb me so much as the Hello Kitty ring of keys laying by one of the teacups. These were my aunt's missing keys.

Suddenly, from behind me, I heard the double kitchen doors swing open. Looking up, there stood a figure about the shape and size of Aunt Xiao-Lin. Below the waist, I recognized her jeans and white

Keds. But her entire upper body was covered in a red tablecloth draped over her head like an opaque crimson veil of a Chinese bride.

"Aunty! Are you ok?"

"How nice of your family to join us for the wedding," a gravely man's voice, decidedly not my aunt's, came out from under the red fabric. I stopped breathing and stepped backwards when I noticed light bounce off the metal cleaver in my aunt's hand as she raised it from beneath the corners of the tablecloth hanging down her sides.

"There's plenty to eat."

My eyes focused on the kitchen cleaver as my aunt walked through the rows of tables and stepped up to the platform. Her path was perfect, as if her eyes were open and uncovered.

"Sit," the voice commanded as the cleaver was raised in my direction.

I sat down in one of the chairs. My aunt sat as well, in the chair across the table from me. I stared at her, at the lumpy shapes poking through the tablecloth where a face would be.

"Do you want to see what's underneath?" The voice asked. My aunt's shoulders seemed to shudder as a whimpering noise emitted from cloth like suppressed laughter or sobbing. "She's prettier now that I've fixed her up. My future wife."

"Aunty, what's going on?" I managed to breathe out, barely audible to my own ears.

Her body slouched against the chair and a loud, hoarse laugh erupted out of the slumped form. "Won't marry me. But . . . ," the voice stopped a moment and my aunt's body suddenly straightened to attention. "You can take her place. I've always liked them young."

I fixed my eyes onto the plate in front of me and bit down hard on my tongue, creating pain to stifle screams.

"Come closer. Pour the tea." My aunt's hand, the one with the cleaver, gestured to the metal teapot.

Everything inside me recoiled at getting closer to whatever was underneath that cloth, but I did not know what else to do. I turned the lazy susan and picked up the metal teapot. My hands shook as I poured cold tea into two tea cups.

"Serve me."

I held my breath and the tea spilled as I fumbled the cup in front of my aunt. Her hand shot out from under the red cloth to wrap like a vice around my wrist.

"Tsk, tsk," the voice said. "Let me teach you how to serve your husband properly." My aunt's hand tightened on my wrist as she raised the cleaver high above her head in her other hand. The intended aim of the blade was unmistakably my hand.

"You can still serve tea with only one hand." The voice laughed.

"Please Aunty! Don't. I'm sorry! You're hurting me," I sobbed and turned my head away, not wanting to see the moment the knife contacted my wrist.

"Don't hurt her. I will agree."

I looked up with relief upon hearing the sweet, soft voice of my aunt. Her real voice that spoke from under the cloth.

"You will marry me? Mine in life and death?" The man's voice came through the cloth again.

"Yes. Let her go."

"Ha! Ha! Ha!" The man laughed, almost uncontrollably, and, even though I was scared, I hated the way he found amusement in our pain. When the laughter finally died down, my aunt's gentle voice urged, "Ruyi, kuai pao." Hurry, run.

"Yes! Run! You can be my second wife when you're bigger." The man began to laugh again as the hold on my hand released.

I wanted to sprint out, back to the car, but I did not want to abandon my aunt to this man of whatever it was. "Aunty, come with me," I pleaded, not knowing how she could leave behind something that controlled her already.

"Kuai, pao," she whispered even as her hand fisted around the raw fish and brought it under the cloth. I heard teeth ripping into the scales and wet flesh. I turned and ran.

"Don't worry, we'll come visit you soon." I heard the voice call after me. Jumping into the car, I scrambled to the floor of the backseat and hid under the reclined passenger seat. I cried and cried, but kept as quiet as I could in case he changed his mind and came to look for me in the car. For hours, I stayed there compressed on folded knees until the rising sun swept layers of reds and oranges over the sky.

That was where my mother found me in the morning, when the police had to break the glass of the car windows to pull me out. At first, she hadn't even known I was there, too preoccupied by the unlocked restaurant, ransacked cash register, and the possibility of a burglar lurking inside. They never found my aunt.

"Missing person, but no evidence of foul play," the Police Report read.

But I know better and, now, you do too. Every night, when I get tired of hiding and want to turn off the lights to sleep, I pull out that slip of paper from the fortune cookie; the one that none of us read before playing the die xian board. The one that I didn't throw away. "Do not walk into the darkness alone." We should have listened.

About Frances Lu-Pai Ippolito

Frances Lu-Pai Ippolito is an emerging Chinese American writer in Portland, Oregon. When she's not spending time with her children in the outdoors, she's crafting short stories in horror, sci-fi, fantasy, or whatever genre-bending she can get away with. Her stories have appeared in Nailed Magazine and HauntedMTL, and will be included in Eerie River Publishing and Black Hare Press's upcoming anthologies. Her work was also recently featured in the Ooligan Press Writers of Color Showcase 2020 in Portland, Oregon.

2

The Butcher's Lunch

CHRIST KENNEDY

They say that the long pig is spreading the latest strain. White, red or pink meat. We have no choice anymore. It's not like it used to be before everybody scattered. People had standards. There was a culture of hygiene but nobody worried that they'd get sick from eating any garden variety anything. If you didn't like meat you'd thrive on quinoa, rye & barley or a thing called dairy. Then, when folks started coughing & dying, those that knew said it was only certain cereals that were making people sick. Our grandparents could trust the government & the whole 'save-my-own-ass' political system only so long as they felt they were safe but, when the first strain hit and neighbours started seeing neighbours dying, no one was certain how it was happening or how long it might last. At first they thought it was terrorists using bio-weapons. World leaders pointed their spindly fingers at each other from across the globe and nations engaged in armed conflicts despite the strain's indiscriminate mind to strike down victims on all sides. While the disease cut through more life than their conventional weapons did military generals urged for the enemy's total destruction by any means. Only the subsequent nuclear Armageddon was able to bring back a semblance of peace.

Then they started saying that it was spreading from the cereals & legumes to the nuts & fruits of tall trees. People around our grandparents thought the radiation from the winds of our ancestors' wars was putting an evil on everything the sun's glance touched. So they rooted out vegetables from the ground and dug up tubers to eat, but even those were tainted with the deadly strain. Famine soon began to compete with Pestilence for the souls of those that went. Of the four horsemen it's only death that profits when pestilence, war, and famine ride about. I know, cause I've seen each come around by and by. Too many people are gone now as the strain takes on more of what's left of our ecosystem. Creatures used to crawl and jump! Believe me, I've seen pictures. Grasses made what stood in the day's breeze green beneath a blue horizon. Now that horizon's a tint of green awash with foul winds and the only thing beneath as far as you can see is the yellow dunes of dirty sand that choke your lungs.

My father's been feeding the maggots for a week now and soon those same maggots we harvest from the diseased bodies won't dilute the strain enough for us to feed our children. It hurts to see your own father pass-on after a lifetime of caring for y'a, but it tears the heart to see the little ones when they first start to cough. You see them choke on their fresh grubs while their tiny hands can barely hang on to the crawly things we eat. Spit comes up out of their irritated throats and that's how you know they're next to go in the pit behind the latrine and the maggot farm. I'm only afraid of the day when the maggots and worms can't feed us anymore so that we'll have to learn to eat sand.

And that's not our worst problem.

Whittled away as we are, there are hunters who are destined to find our lair, but now they say that the long pig is spreading the latest strain. So at least we can fight back even while our babies scream out for help from within the mythical lion's hale jaw. A suckling babe's as potent as the bravest warrior, but I'll not pay for my life with my son's, so I am off to find the butcher who strays away from his people's oases and hunts about in our dunes. Make a bargain and bring him to market to get a better price for the lives of my family.

Now, after days of trailing his scent, I've finally found him. The bold nimrod whose avarice so asserts itself he can't stop from hunting members of his own party until he alone returns from the hunt friendless, fat, feasted and fed. He hunts alone now while I track him, ready to pounce and invite Death to his door. The few maggots I still have will give me strength but it's the potency of the blemished pink flesh that will destroy him and his kind. Now, with my father's hand to bless me, this lone hunter will lead me to know the gates of our enemies and they may yet never know ours. I feel the bile of my hate rise as loathing overwhelms my senses and catches at my craw. Taking gulps of what water I have to force the putrid meat down, my eyes never lose sight of the prey as he approaches the dune behind which I lay in ambush waiting for his approach. With the last of the meat safely past my chafing throat, I stifle the urge to eject the bane which I've armed myself with and wait patiently for the moment to stand and charge at the butcher as he nears.

My stomach cries for relief from the pain it endures as my feet stumble over the dune. Each step jolts the ordnance in my bowels and prepares to launch the attack that will slay the nation which threatens my son's crib, haunts my wife's cot and prepares to set itself against my neighbour's kin. Leagues away from the gates I hope to batter for my kind, I sally forth at the Butcher who now towers over me at arms reach. He deftly parries my first weak shot and I launch at him anew. Ably deflecting my fumbling attack with his gauntleted hands, he counters with his own and quickly quashes my next feint before throwing me to the ground. With renewed vigour, I grapple at his leg and gnaw at its thick, burly calf with the venom of my bile while I lay in the hot sands that my own blood reddens beneath me during the endless seconds it takes for this Butcher to shackle my elbows behind my back.

As the virulence of my vital fluids now mixes with the Butcher's blood and taints my broken, yellow teeth, I feel the acrid taste of it irritating my already sensitive throat and I repress a cough to hush all evidence of my method. The Butcher sneers down at me a moment while pressing his heavy boot on my chest, which churns up the bitter acerbic fruits of my spleen that lick at the edges of my angry palate. He quickly darts away looking for more of my kind, certain I couldn't have been fool enough to attack him without assistance. After he has carefully climbed the next dune and peered across the sands at the green tinted horizon, he returns to his pack assured there was no body of victuals other than my own.

"Ah, English," he says with a broad smile, "you can't know how well you blessed me."

After a pause of quiet reflection, he then ceremoniously kneels before me where I lay on the burning sand pinioned and trussed--waiting as he prepares to make a consecration to the God that created this world of misery. Gathering dried fuels from his parcels, he takes the first choice that fits neatly in his scarred hand, then squats down beside it and strikes his coruscating flint with the worn edge of a long rusted nail until a spark ignites the precious desiccated fecal nugget he uses to give thanks for his bounty. Vainly struggling, I let off a quiet, despairing moan, miming the tones needed to lure my prey into docility. Whispering quietly between himself and his God, he lets his dirt encrusted eyelids slide down over his large grey eyes until barely a slither remains open through which he stares intently at the gift he has received. His prayer complete, he unsheathes the knife that never strays far from his hand and, with a knee pressed heavily on my chest, pinches my nose tightly before severing it from my body with one swift agonizing slice.

As I cry out for the injustice, that only a God cruel enough to create this dejected world may allow, I watch him gently place the Lord's offering on the burning fuel and bow his head in prayer. Feeling the burning of its flames where the knife had branded me chattel and fleeced me of my freedom, I freely give myself into the Butcher's hands in order to save my loved ones. Once the proudest warrior of my tribe, I now lay as a lamb at the feet of a foreign invader eager still to know the gates of his people.

When he has completed his rite, he lays the blood tainted blade of his knife onto the hot flames and busies himself with his pack before returning to it again. His attention on me now, he gives me a hearty smile and clasps my neck affectionately before pressing the red glow of his knife against the stump of my nose to squelch the bleeding.

"You know your part now, English?" he asks as he cleans his knife and waits for me to speak.

"You and your kind will never return here," I state plainly through a blood choked throat that projects my voice in a hoarser tone than I am accustomed to hear.

"Yes, yes, English, that's right," he agrees mockingly, "it was evident in your attack that you have the means to threaten both me AND my kind."

I vainly sputter to clear the nostrils I no longer have and send blood bubbles down my chin as he pulls me to my feet. The fierce look of malice I let escape from me would have made a wiser prey more wary but this heedless fool guffaws at my determination and clasps my shoulder as he laughs obliviously before me. Wiping tears of mirth from his eyes, he shoves me along with a command to march as he takes up his pack and follows close behind.

"We're going to market, English," he informs me, "and you don't need to worry. I'll sell you whole and we'll be parted."

"The parting is not what worries me," I struggle to speak through the blood that continues to pour down the callously cauterized gash above my mouth. "I'm more concerned for you and yours."

"Enough with the comedy," he says wearily, "we've a long walk."

I stumble with his first shove, then steady myself and continue apace among the indistinct dunes sensing the bounds straining at my elbows that pull my shoulders back with the ardent pride I feel for having already reached this milestone.

"Your people go to market on a day such as this?" I ask referring to the desert storm winds that kick up sand at our feet and blast painfully at my open wound.

"Each market has its day," he replies with confidence, "so march as I tell you and we'll join today's market before long. Soon you'll be rid of me and I of you. If you make no fuss, I'll be easy on you and sell you whole."

"Be easy or be hard," I reply, concealing my passion. "It'll be right with me either way."

"Breach my trust and I will be hard," he promises as he yanks on the tether that binds him to me. His muffled voice reaches across the sand strewed air through the scarf he has carefully wrapped around his head to protect him from the caustic winds while I plunge forward tilting my bleeding face towards the lee of the gathering storm's worst ravages. I hear him chortle to himself about my stupidity as he gently shoves me along the shifting dunes to an end he does not yet understand.

As the sands impair my ability to see, I march on, wincing from the pain the winds bring me, and focus my mind on the face of my young son whose life is now balanced against mine. My eyes are fused shut by the storm as I begin to perceive the voices of distant relatives calling to me from the strands of a far off shore. Thanking me for my sacrifice, their urgent pleas for refuge from harm push me forward as my valour battles with insurmountable forces. Still, I press on until their cries dissipate and meld into an inchoate babble that vacillates incomprehensibly into the faint but coherent coloquy we are approaching. At last, the winds abate and I can hear their voices clearly now that we stand within their midst. I struggle to open my eyes and finally see the market gate I have long sought to destroy.

Keeping my eyes from the sun's burning glare, I squint to see the goings on around me and detect the shadow of the man tied to my tether as he nervously negotiates his entry fee with the armed guard who bars our way. They haggle a price deemed sufficient by the soldier but begrudged by the abashed merchant who turns to me to exact the duty. Unsheathing his knife, he pulls his tether to lead me to the toll counter. The tie that binds my elbows limits the flexibility in my arms so he tugs at me and shoves me into place then prepares to collect the soldier's due. Struggling to facilitate the endeavour, he twists my left arm until it breaks and I let out a cry despite my attempts to stifle the pain, knowing it is for my son that I allow this to happen. With my arm broken, my forearm is readily placed onto the sturdy counter and the teeth of a dull saw hack at the flesh above my left wrist. A gag is thrown into my mouth and I bite into it until the grating motion of the blade stops and the Butcher is forced to let me drop where I fall.

I listen to the banter they exchange. They laugh and trade insults pleasantly, each one goading the other with a smirk until they part and the Butcher turns his attention to me.

"Alright, English," he says. "Not quite whole, but I can still sell you quickly and be on my way." He stoops beside me and shoves me to my side so he can inspect the work he's done. When the tourniquet he has tied around my stump passes inspection he lifts me by the armpits and stands me on my feet.

"Now don't make trouble here, English, or I'll make it hard for you," he sneers in my face as the pain forces me to cringe and turn away my eyes humbled by the torment. "Breach my trust now and I'll barter your toes for a bag of salt and we'll see how you stand then."

He cuffs the back of my head, but the blow deflects senselessly off his seasoned knuckles and I stagger on where our tether leads me. We jostle through the crowd as I see more chattel who, like me, are being gathered to the fresh meat quarter. The Butcher takes possession of a blood encrusted stump on which to carry on the day's business. He pushes the backs of my knees as he guides me to the ground and I land in a heap beside the rotten lumber and listen to the gaggle of the market as families pass by, bleary eyed and bored, hungry or tired, scanning over the produce on offer. He prepares a small fire as the crowds mull around and gather, going about their business. Some hold coins in their hands, looking for a bargain, while others have servants to assist them in their shopping. The haggling starts but the Butcher turns away the first bidder with insults then deals with a pleasant old woman who holds out the few coins she has and asks for what he can give her.

"Will you take his mouth," he offers as he pinches my lips to show her how thick the meat is.

"I have a hungry boy," she says trying to get a better trade, "I'll need both his tongue and lips."

"Deal," he says and his knife is quickly unsheathed. Ripping off the flesh from around my lips, he is generous and carves into my cheeks in sympathy for the good widow.

"Oh my," she says, "he is a screamer, isn't he."

"Fresh meat, ma'am, can't be helped," his assurances quell her concerns as she prepares to receive her purchase.

With my face bleeding freely now, he pulls my head back over the stump on which I am leaning and reaches inside with the pliers he keeps handy in his pocket. Once my severed tongue is in her hands and he has taken her coins, he holds a glowing ember with his tongs and, jamming it into and around my mouth, stems the bleeding. A cloth is promptly fitted into my blood-streaming maw and stifles my screams as children laugh and point while their parents lead them away with a sneer of contempt for my poor behavior. My breath bubbles in rivulets of gore that quickly soak the cloth. I gag and choke as my parched throat forces me to cough and a spray of jettisoned red phlegm smears itself over the Butcher's boots just as another customer arrives. He is a lean man with an honest face, hands that work stone or labour in a mine. I despair to see my son and abandon my present state to live in an ethereal realm where pain is but a murmur of hope and death is only a long needed rest, but I am brought back to my torment without further chance for escape.

Butcher unties my elbows and lays my right arm across the block.

"No," I scream vainly through the blood drenched cloth in my mouth as he ties the tourniquet then haggles with the buyer for more money before lowering the string further down along my arm.

He stands and they argue until the customer feigns to walk away with his final insult, then relents and drops another coin into the Butcher's hand and my arm is deftly tied with a fine string over my collar bone. He holds my head away from the blade as I am tempted and try to lean in for the stroke that will release me. As he saws off my arm, I watch the buyer prepare a sackcloth to take home his purchase. The arm that once held my young son safe to my chest, that gave support to my ailing wife and that bore the hammer for unending hours of toil falls silently into the blood stained sack and swings casually in the honest man's hands until the crowds billow around him like waves over a sunken relic.

Abandoned to my reverie I find myself lost in the drizzle of a cooling rain near the plashing trickle of a clear stream. My wife coos amorously at me as she rubs her swollen belly and watches our active son bounding from verdant bush to cerulean stream as the din of the market echoes, only faintly now, in my recollection until the stream's color reflects the sky's ruby crimson and I am once again recalled to my harrowing distress and torture. I see Butcher doing his work, but I am numb to the pain. As my body writhes beneath him, I in my mind watch from a safe distance above the market. He banters pleasantly with his patron who smiles appreciably and folds a cloth over the doted cut of meat, then diligently places it in his bag beneath a prized jar of honey and some tobacco he may share with a friend after his wife has served their market day feast. I hear his thoughts as the pleasant memory of an evening with family and guests for a delicious roast cooked like only his wife knows how inhabits the honest patron's uncluttered mind.

I begin to suspect Butcher has given me medication to relieve me from the pain since I first embarrassed him in the eyes of the market patrons. He laughs despite himself as he counts the coins in his pocket and makes a mental tally of my worth. I hear the soft tinkling of his coins bounce and jostle together at the bottom of his purse. As the shoppers begin to dwindle and there is little hope for further business, he considers whether he should feast on my thigh and carry me to the next market or settle for what blood he can gather without further damaging his merchandise. Having made up his mind to do what's best for his purse, he holds a large cup beneath the stump of my left arm and loosens the tourniquet until it is full. The discomfort of his actions do not pierce through me as they did before and only a numbing sensation reaches the nerve endings in my head now as I lay on a cushion of adored recollections beneath a warm cloak of tender amity for the people I have left behind.

"We have a long walk ahead of us, English," he says in a brusque voice. "Don't make me be hard on you."

His tone is friendly but menacing, though I am not sure what he means with this threat since I am quite numb to anything he may do now. As my mind struggles to imagine the substance of his decree, he drinks the cup of my lifeblood in peace, letting his mind rest from the long day of haggling. Soon he is done and brings me to my feet, then kindly holds me to be certain I don't stagger to the ground. The rope that ties him to me is wrapped around my waist now and I lead him away from the empty market towards the gates that I now know better than any of my kin before me. The winds have died down and I can no longer feel the sands that blasted into my martyred face as I did just hours before. He points me in the right direction as we pass through the gate and we wander through the desert a short distance to the next market. I no longer feel time as it slides away behind me like waters lapping quietly on the banks of the same genial stream. Awake only in the sense that perception grants me glimpses into the real world, I am not conscious enough to grasp at the intricacies of reality that overwhelm my failing faculties.

I see myself stumbling as I walk and it is only after falling for the third time that Butcher finally takes me over his shoulders and holds me as a shepherd may hold a lost lamb across his shoulders. The sand sticks to my wounds and my companion has no time to wipe it off. Soon we are at another market and the tourniquet is moved up my leg in discrete steps that can only be quantized by the weight of coins tinkling at the bottom of the Butcher's purse. Soon I am a lump and a head bereft of limbs and free to fly above the pain of existence as I watch from my eyrie of awareness high above the common man, the patrons and the Butcher. The market closes and I am thrust inside a sack slung over his shoulder. My head protrudes from it's peak and I press my throat against a taut leather cord but life refuses to ebb from me still. Too weak to pursue this through to its end, I am forced to bow my head in subjection to the ignominy of my position beneath the sun's fiery desert air. The gag in my mouth has dried to a crust and my parched throat refuses to swallow what bile I may have mixed with my pestilent blood.

The Butcher struggles for breath beneath me as he walks but remains steady in his pace until I look into his mind's eye and see the market approaching ahead. My eyes are closed, but the severity of my psychotic throes give me a clarity I have never had. A placid derangement has washed over me and I am released from the discomforts of the physical human existence I once clung to. Finally, I open my eyes and see the darkness abright with warriors of my kin's past in seraphic lights above me. The lustre of their swords raised high for our enemies to see, I close them again and prepare for the astral voyage that will rapture me into the ranks of the proud martyred soldiers of my clan.

Soon I am jostled awake as Butcher throws down his packs.

"We'll camp here tonight, English," he says.

He squats next to me to inspect my condition then, satisfied that I may live until morning, he opens his packs and prepares his camp. Starting a fire in his usual manner, he rolls his bundle and places it on the ground nearby then picks me up and lays me on my belly with the bundle, raising my hips. He tears at my loincloth and in moments he is jabbing his weapon inside me and I feel the hot boiling pain thrust my innards and jostle the bane that now travels with my limbs to afflict those who would hurt my kin. When he is done, he callously tugs at his bundle and rolls over in a huff of exhausted satisfaction and slaps me on the buttocks laughing out loudly.

"Ahhh, English, you don't know how much joy you bring me!"

He is soon ready to feast and rolls me on my back. The flames of his fire dance in the darkness as the cooling air whistles his contentment. His knife in hand, he easily severs my manhood and thrusts it upon his blade, then inspects it briefly.

"A minor feast," he says with relish and looks down at my charred breathing carcass with a tinge of pride.

Letting his meal slowly roast over the flame, he takes out his purse then counts and inspects each coin with the peace of mind of a pleased nabob. Soon he is ready for his collation, but he stops himself with a mirthful smile directed at me. Holding the smouldering appendage close to his mouth, he mockingly fellates his meal then guffaws with delight.

"Does that feel good, English?"

I watch from above and see his humour as a facade for a pain he hides with difficulty. Still he relishes his meal and slurps at the blood that trickles down his chin then smears his dirty sleeve across his face before wiping down his blade and sheathing it. When he is done, I am told to get some rest for the long day ahead. I watch him pull a blanket over himself and roll over. A moment later his thoughts are slow but cruel, maniacal and intemperate. He is asleep. His mind disturbs me more in the shuddering rest of night than during his long hours of deliberate daylight malice.

An hour passes as I watch his fitful mind before he begins to cough. At first only once, and then a second hearty cough rattles the electricity in his head. Soon a violent slew of hacking and spitting awakens him. He urgently pushes himself off the ground and reaches for his gourd as he holds his breath before another series of convulsive shocks jolt his chest and force the bane of my father's blood through the arteries of his brain. Shortly he is relieved enough to take a drink from his gourd and, in the lull of that moment, my own merry convulsions draw his attention to me. Holding up a white cloth to my face so as to reflect the light of the swords of my kin upon it allows him to read the mirth of joy that washes over my eyes. Falling backwards onto his scattered bundle, he spills his water and lays on his side, seething violently at the thought of a long pig laughing at his plight. Fitful kicks jerk furiously from him for a moment then cease along with his breath and only the glowing embers of his dying fire remain when the soft tinkling of his purse subsides.

About Christ Kennedy

As a French Quebecois who failed English Lit. in 11th grade, he is now proud to own enough Air-Guitars and Bugbear bait & growth hormones to fill imagination's warehouse. He steals the manners of fools to feed his pen then writes what prose the Muses could only plagiarize. Sesquipedaliating whenever he neologisticates he keeps a "unique word count" as a benchmark and lets rhythm flow into his prose.

With a Bachelor of Engineering as a tool to guide him he is developing the science of theological engineering into an iconoclastic art of reason.

Also by Christ Kennedy

The People : A Novel by Christ Kennedy

Two Sons Nelson, Nomad : Sequel to Two Sons Nelson

Cleats of the Counter Revolution

Paladin : An Origin Story

3

Dapper Man

DAVID LANGE

It was a beautiful October day and I couldn't have asked for a better stage to show off my beloved Manhattan to a couple friends whose lives were sadly unfulfilled, never having experienced the splendor of a Big Apple autumn. Cynthia and "Don't Call Me Chuck" Charles were classmates from USC and stayed local, both finding jobs in the Los Angeles area, following graduation. I had actually dated Cynthia during my first year in college and I was convinced we had something going. Then I moved on. Actually, "Cynth" moved on . . . and I waited a year or two before I decided I would, too. We stayed friends, neither of us wanting to part with the good vibes or wonderful conversations that made our platonic bond so uniquely special. Charles transferred in during our Junior year and his larger than life personality immediately attracted Cynthia. I convinced myself that I was happy for the two of them and supportive of their growing intimacy. A real friendship blossomed between the three of us and I willingly joined in on outings and touring excursions. Cynthia and Charles always did their best to make me not feel like a third wheel. If I had only let go sooner, I might have found my peace. Instead, I will forever be haunted by the day I met the stranger . . . the day we all met The Dapper Man.

With only the three-day Columbus Day weekend to work with, I developed a rather aggressive touring schedule for my friends and they were game for all of it. Empire State Building, Statue of Liberty, Times Square, China Town, a few museums, and, of course, the beauty of Central Park; the leaves were bursting out in brilliant hues of autumnal glory—oranges, reds, yellows; even purple. A smattering of fallen leaves made a lovely crunching sound beneath our feet as we walked the paths throughout the park. Up ahead, in a clearing, several performers took advantage of the favorable climate to earn a few more tips before the cold winds of November drove them from the park. We sat on a park bench and listened to a guitarist who did some very nice renditions of several Beatles songs. When he started to repeat his four-song set, I knew it was time to move on. I walked over and dropped a five into his guitar case. Charles joked that it was worth only a buck-fifty, at best. It was really worth $10, or better, but I didn't have that kind of money as a junior associate with my company; a guy trying to scrape by in one of the most expensive cities on the planet, $5 would have to do.

A street mime approached Cynthia and re-enacted a strike to the heart from Cupid's arrow followed by the gracious gifting of an invisible rose to our lovely friend. We all got a kick out of that and Charles insisted we get our photo taken with the mime. He was good about it. I would have preferred we just got on our way. The mime acted out the motions of wiping a tear from his eye as we left. Photo and all, we really should have given him some money. I was running low but it was clear that my travel companions weren't about to cough up any dough. I turned around and ran back to give the mime a five-dollar bill. I had nothing left now but a couple twenties.

We continued to walk the path on the outskirts of an open field. The sky was a magnificent sapphire blue and several picture-perfect fluffy clouds slowly drifted across the scene, in no hurry to reach their final destination. Artists only dream of recreating this kind of splendor upon the canvas.

Out ahead, just before our path re-entered a wooded section of the park, there appeared a finely dressed man who, upon closer inspection, seemed like something out of a 1930s musical. As we drew nearer, we heard the distinct tapping of his tap shoes upon the pavement. He was an older gentleman but cut an elegant figure in his black full-dress tailcoat tuxedo, white gloves, top hat, and dancing cane. Occasionally, he would stumble a bit as his knee seemed to give way, attempting to land a twirling jump or recover from a dramatic leap off the nearby park bench which he expertly incorporated into his routine. Several older women and one couple, who I imagined to be newlyweds on their honeymoon, applauded the dancer as he performed for them. Cynthia was very interested so we decided to stop for a bit to watch. The dancer tipped his hat, acknowledging us. Invigorated by the growing audience, he seemed to step up his game—throwing in even more daring dance moves. The theatrical makeup which was now clearly visible upon his face did little to conceal the wrinkles that betrayed his true age. Cynthia was spellbound but Charles was growing increasingly impatient. He'd clearly had enough of street corner musicians, mimes, and dancers and was eager to find a place where he could grab a couple beers. "Hey Cynthia, let's snap a couple pics and get going, I'm getting thirsty and Pat promised he'd buy the first round." I had made no such promise.

"Come on, Charles, let's just watch for a bit. This guy is really good." Cynthia tried the nice approach first. She always does.

"Um, hello, Earth to Cynthia. We came here to feel the vibe of the City, not to watch a washed-up Broadway bit player stumble over himself." Charles spoke a little too loudly and the old ladies gave him an angry glare. We were rapidly becoming unwelcome interlopers on their excursion down memory lane. Worse yet, I think the dancing gentleman may have heard, too. He looked over briefly, following Charles' rude comment, but, rather than taking offense, he re-doubled his efforts to put on a good show. Unfortunately, his knee buckled as he leaped up onto the park bench and he flipped over the backrest and crashed spectacularly on the grass behind. The poor old ladies gasped and the bride softly uttered a concerned "Oh no!" Charles was less sympathetic.

"Dude, you should not be dancing at your age. Does your insurance even cover death by dance?" Cynthia and I walked over to see if we could help the man up but Charles just pulled out his phone and filmed the poor fellow as he tried to pull himself up using the bench as an aid. Charles couldn't stop laughing as he embarked upon the creation of a video clip he hoped would go viral on YouTube before the night was over. Worse yet, he added in his own condescending narrative. "We're here in New York City's Central park where the Ghost of Fred Astaire has just completed the spectacular debut of his new production aptly entitled 'Fall in New York.' The question on everyone's mind is whether or not all the king's horses and all the king's men can ever put Humpty Dancer together again?"

"Stop it, Charles. That's not cool. I think he's hurt." Cynthia always was the compassionate one. I think the dancer was hurt, but he refused to take my outstretched hand. Instead, he eventually returned to his feet under his own power. There were distinct mud stains upon his lapel and on both of his trouser legs. The man was visibly shaken. His hand trembled as he pulled out his handkerchief and began to address the mud. Charles came closer, still filming until Cynthia literally yelled at him "turn that damn thing off, already! Let the poor guy have his dignity."

Almost imperceptibly, at first, the clouds seemed to cease their peaceful ambling and, instead, conspired most purposefully to blot out thc sun. An eerie overcast subsumed the park. Charles certainly picked up on the emotion in Cynthia's voice but completely missed the disgusted looks of the attending audience. "Okay. Sorry. Let's snap a couple pics and then let the assisted living facility take care of Uncle Charlie here." Charles grabbed the dancer and pulled him in close to take a few "selfies" with the old man. "Say Cheez—y dance routine." Cynthia just shook her head, fighting back a few tears. I urged Charles to stop and come with us.

"Come on, Charles; first round's on me, remember?"

"Okay, okay, I'm coming. This dude ain't gonna smile no matter how hard I try. Hey, Fred, what's your real name? I want to make sure you get credit when this video wins an award." The man said nothing. He did his best to ignore Charles but our friend kept taunting. "Can you even talk or are you like from the silent movie era? You should get together with the mime on the other side of the park—you guys would have some rockin' conversations."

The dancer turned back towards his audience and started to dance again but he barely got a few steps in before his leg completely folded under him and he fell on the pavement, scraping his chin and nose upon impact. He stumbled to his feet only to fall again. Charles was filming it all on his phone. "Ladies and gentleman, turn off the stage lights, this show is over."

Tears were rolling down the cheeks of the two older women. They both walked over and left some money in his top hat, laying on the ground beside him. They waited to make sure he was able to return to his feet. Well, Charles was right, the dancing was done for the day. The young couple also placed a generous tip in the old man's hat before they turned to walk away. The skies seemed to be darkening ominously and a strong wind created an unpleasant chill in the air. I could see the bride covering herself with a sweater as the groom ushered her away from the scene. With his audience departed, the old dancer stood there, trembling, and looking very unsteady. Were it not for his cane, now operating as a functional third leg, I'm not sure he would have kept his balance. Charles seemed unmoved and motioned for us to be on our way. "Let's get going, there's nothing more to see here and I think the old fella's going to be just fine." Charles turned away and began walking. Cynthia was clearly troubled but was struggling to find a remedy beyond a nearly inaudible inquiry as to the man's health. The inquiry, if heard, was never answered. I reached back for my wallet and slowly approached the dancer. When I opened my wallet, I remembered that I had given away my smaller bills earlier in the day. I felt very badly but I wasn't about to drop a twenty-dollar tip for a few minutes of dancing.

"I'm sorry. I'm out of cash. We really enjoyed the show. Thanks. Um . . . bye." I ran to catch up with Charles and Cynthia. "Hey, Cynth, do you happen to have a fiver on you? I think we really ought to tip that guy. Cynthia shrugged.

"Sorry, Pat, all I've got is plastic today." Charles made a silly face and shook his head.

"Maybe he's got a card reader in his pocket? I'm guessing grandpa isn't going to fare well with a PayPal transfer." Cynthia shot an angry look over at Charles.

"Seriously, dude, you need to chill. I hope that poor guy has a nice home somewhere near and a family to go home to. I feel really badly for him." Charles was unmoved.

"He's probably like some Wall Street mogul who just does this for kicks on the weekend. He does remind me a bit of Mr. Monopoly—well, without the mustache that is. Okay, Pat, set us on a course for the nearest watering hole." As we walked, the old man's eyes never left us.

Even though it was only late afternoon, the lights were already coming on in the park and the winds were howling. This change in weather is not something the forecast had warned of. Before making a direct line for a park exit, I led my companions through a colorful forested pathway so that they could further appreciate the glory of the fall leaves which, unfortunately, were losing some of their vibrancy in the dimming light. With no other park goers in sight, I began to feel a bit uneasy. My anxiety was clearly not shared by my companions who had no memories of perilous nighttime crossings through Central Park in the darkness. I had a few unpleasant experiences during my younger days that stayed with me through the years. My senses were now on high alert. Up ahead, I saw a shadowy figure leaning against a lamp post. Cynthia and Charles kept gabbing away like unwitting tourists but I slowly placed my hands in my pockets and quietly assessed the situation as we approached. My heart all but stopped when I realized it was him . . . the dancing man. How did he even get here? A second or so later, Charles and Cynthia identified the man and they, too, got quiet. Charles just laughed. "Yeah! Encore." He jogged down the pathway to where the gentleman stood. Cynthia began to mutter the words "Please stop," but never got past a mumbled first syllable. Then, much to our horror, Charles took the man's hat and placed it on his head. He also grabbed his dancing cane and started to perform an outrageously silly routine.

"Charles, what the Hell are you doing? Cut that shit out!" He wasn't listening. Charles was lost in his own self-centered world and having the time of his life. Cynth and I walked at an increasingly rapid pace towards where the scene was playing out. The wind was really blowing now and it blew the cap off of Charles' head and carried it down the pathway where it rested at the feet of the old man. His eyes were burning with rage. The violence of the wind, now whipping the tree limbs to and fro, seemed to reflect the intensity of the anger of this once gentle man.

When Charles walked over and offered the cane back, Cynthia and I breathed a deep sigh of relief. And then our jerky friend quickly pulled the cane back and taunted "You didn't say please." The old dancer carefully replaced his top hat which somehow withstood the tremendous winds that should have carried it all the way to 5th Avenue or, more likely, the East River. He was trembling with rage as he outstretched his hand to reach for his cane. Once more, Charles pretended to offer it up, only to pull it back. The old dancer's body shuttered frighteningly, as if some demon had possessed his spirit, and he let loose the most horrifically blood-curdling shriek imaginable. This ungodly utterance was unlike anything I had ever heard . . . not even within my worst nightmares. So thunderous was this cry that hundreds of jet-black crows, frightened from their resting perches in the branches above, took to the air with an equally disconcerting chorus of frantic cawing. Charles' face went pale and he dropped the cane where he stood. He stepped back a few paces, still visibly in shock. The old man lithely bent over to retrieve his cane; his face now expressionless. Charles quickly returned to us. No longer the class clown, he seemed dead serious about quickly finding an exit to the park. Our once pleasant stroll along the wooded paths of Central Park had become a frightening excursion into darkness. We reversed our course and backtracked along the route we had taken until I got my bearings. I have to admit, I was panicking a bit and decided to head off the path and make a direct line east towards the edge of the park. No words were spoken as we negotiated the hills, rocks, and trees that stood between us and the safety of 5th Avenue. The familiar sounds of traffic could not have been more welcome. We all took a deep breath when buildings and cars appeared through the trees. Charles and I helped Cynthia up over the stone wall that was our only remaining barrier. Once over the wall, we all looked at each other and laughed, albeit nervously. Catching her breath, Cynthia asked "What the Hell happened in there?" I just shook my head.

"No freakin' idea. Are you guys still up for some drinks?" Charles still wasn't talking but he nodded his head and gave me a thumbs up. We had hardly walked ten paces down the sidewalk when a rather disheveled homeless man approached us. He was wearing a torn Army field jacket and some baggy pants that must have been three sizes too big for him. His hair was completely white as was his unkempt beard. Charles and Cynthia weren't as used to seeing homeless people so they withdrew back a few steps leaving me to do the talking. "Sorry man. Got nothing for you today." The man looked at me with an expression of annoyance upon his wrinkled face.

"I didn't ask for no money, young man." I immediately felt guilty.

"I'm really sorry. I didn't mean to . . ." Before I could complete my sentence, the man lost interest and walked right past me until he stood directly in front of Charles. Charles took another step back, repulsed by the appearance and odor of the unfortunate drifter standing before him. The retreat offered him no reprieve—the old fellow just closed the gap once more. He stared into Charles' eyes with a disturbing intensity.

"What are you looking at?!" asked Charles. He was now posturing in an attempt to intimidate the aging vagrant. The homeless man was not intimidated. He just shook his head and laughed.

"Mmmm mmmm, you shouldna fucked with Dapper Man." All the color left Charles' face.

"What?" asked Charles, confusion and fear robbing him of his confidence.

"Dapper Man. You . . . should . . . not have . . . fucked . . . with . . . Dapper Man. Nothin' good ever comes from fuckin' with Dapper Man. You're gonna regret it, son. I don't need your money. I'm just thanking the good Lord that I ain't in your shoes." He laughed again and gave a half-hearted salute as he turned to walk away, mumbling as he went. "You all have a good evening now. Enjoy the Big Apple." We could faintly hear him humming the New York, New York song as he slowly trudged away. We stood there quietly, for a while. Cynthia nervously tried to reassure us all.

"He must have seen us with that dancing guy. He was kind of dapper. Well, at first. That crazy, primal, scream-thing kind of freaked me out but, hey, he was a little upset so . . ."

"Have you ever heard anyone scream like that, Cynth," I asked. "I mean, ever?"

"Okay. Well, let's put that in the past. We could have been nicer to the old guy but it's not like we committed any heinous act of inhumanity." Charles agreed with Cynthia.

"Right, I was just having some fun with the old guy. The mime didn't seem to have an issue with a little bit of fun so why should this Dapper Guy?" I feigned my best serious look, just to mess with Charles."

"Dapper Man, Charles. His name is The Dapper Man." Charles seemed somewhat taken aback. Mission accomplished! I finally cracked a smile and the game was up. We all started laughing as we turned back up the street, on our way to Tabby's Bistro for some drinks. The place had a good atmosphere and I knew it was just what the doctor ordered to set the stage for some more fun in the City.

With drinks in hand and a platter of Tabby's Deluxe Nachos to share, the mirth and frivolity was rekindled. Memories of many happy outings in California came flooding back. My head was in a good place. In the spirit of the conversation, I fired off a great zinger at Charles, waiting for some approving laughter and more than ready to respond to his counter attack. I was met by silence. I repeated my joke. Had it somehow offended my friends? My mind was reevaluating the last twenty seconds when I noticed that both

Charles and Cynthia were no longer looking at me but had their gazes fixed directly towards a street light across the road. My distance vision wasn't quite what it was a few years ago so I squinted to try to make out the details of the scene. I joined my comrades in stunned silence when the unmistakable figure of Dapper Man materialized at the very outskirts of the soft glow of the street lamp. Inside the well-lit bistro, we must have shone like a beacon to all passersby. And, just like that, my appetite was gone. We were all feeling very uneasy but Cynthia was the first to express our shared concern.

"Okay, now this is getting a little creepy. Let's say we just get the check and head on down to Times Square, as you recommended. Pat, are you listening?" I was listening, but it took me a few seconds to process Cynthia's words as my mind was elsewhere.

"Yah, right. Great idea. I doubt he's following us but I'm all for putting more space between us and that Dapper Guy."

"Dapper Man!" Charles replied, winking.

"Right. Dapper Man." I raised my arm and gave a quick wave to our waitress to signal her that we were ready for our check." A few minutes later, the waitress arrived and handed us the check. Cynthia quickly snatched it.

"This one's on me." She smiled and turned the check over to assess the damage. Her smile disappeared completely and her eyes widened.

"That much?" I joked. Cynthia held the check so that we might all see it clearly. Written in bold red letters across the paper were the unmistakable words "Dapper Man does not suffer fools gladly." Charles' reaction was immediate. He yelled across the bistro for the waitress and she signaled that she'd be over momentarily. Once she had finished with the table she was attending, the waitress came over to see what we needed.

"Anything wrong with the bill, Sir?"

"Not with the bill," responded Charles, angrily, "but I'd like an explanation about this!" Charles menacingly outstretched his arm until our check was only six inches from the waitress' eyes. She backed away, a concerned look upon her face.

"Oh, that," she responded calmly, trying to defuse the situation. "It's simple really." She paused as she considered her words. "It means you shouldn't screw with Dapper Man. Ever." A voice from across the establishment called out for more coffee and our waitress politely excused herself. Charles was clearly not satisfied. He yelled out across the restaurant.

"This is a bunch of BS!" Charles was about to head after the waitress but Cynthia grabbed his arm, motioning with her head that we should just head out. "Okay. Let's go. But no tip. Nothing."

We hastily departed Tabby's and stopped briefly to look across the street. Dapper Man was gone. With my friends in tow, I headed for the 96th Street station to catch a downtown train. The crowded street provided me with a reassuring sense of comfort and safety that I'm not sure my friends shared. Using my MetroCard, I swiped Charles and Cynthia through the turnstile and continued leading them towards the downtown platform. Even though I was used to waiting on subways, on this night, every minute seemed excruciating. I kept looking at the stairs, half expecting Dapper Man to make an appearance. Charles and Cynthia didn't say a word but I know my friends were uneasy, as well. Once on the train, I took a deep breath and slowly exhaled. I hardly noticed the stench of urine and vomit that permeated the car. 86th Street. 77th Street. 68th Street, Hunter College. I mentally checked off the stops as we made our way south on the island. At 68th Street, our car emptied. This early in the evening, on a holiday weekend, the sudden departure of our fellow riders seemed unusual—the emptiness seized my attention. I didn't want to alarm Charles or

Cynthia so I didn't say a thing. Charles looked at me and smiled, joking that it was about time we got some room to stretch out. Cynthia asked if we might move down a bit, away from the horrible smell. I nodded but I was fairly certain that the entire car wreaked of human excretions. The subway doors closed and we slowly pulled away from the station.

When our train arrived at the 59th Street station, my heart rate went up exponentially—the station appeared to be completely abandoned. Despite this, the train remained stationary, its car doors open. Cynthia let out a terrified shriek and pointed towards one of the support pillars. Standing beside the steel support beam, as straight and erect as the pillar itself, was the Dapper Man. His lifeless eyes and expressionless face added to his terrifying visage. Slowly, he began to walk towards us. Cynthia was completely freaking out at this point, screaming that we needed to get out of the train and leave the station. Despite our combined prayers, the doors remained open and the train motionless. I choked on my words as I bid my friends to follow me. We raced to one end of the car and through the doors into the next car. I peeked out the window and Dapper Man was still approaching the train. We hurried through two more cars, all abandoned. There was something terribly unnatural about the scene but the only thing on my mind was putting some distance between us and the Dapper Man. I poked my head out of one of the doors just in time to see the Dapper Man entering the car we had previously been riding in.

"Quick, let's get out!" I shouted. Before I could even take a step towards the car's exit, the doors whooshed shut with incredible speed. "Shit!" I was rapidly assessing the situation. Looking through the scratched little window at the end of the car, I was fairly certain I saw some motion from a few cars down. Was Dapper Man coming towards us? My fears were realized when I saw the door open between the car behind us and its predecessor. Dapper Man was slowly ambling our way, still somewhat unsteady on his feet. "Let's go!" We quickly moved forward through the cars. I was fairly confident that we would reach the next stop, at 51st Street, before Dapper Man could reach us. We did. The train slowly rolled into the station and stopped at the platform. And we waited. The doors did not open. I yelled as loud as I could, hoping the train operator might hear me, "Please open the doors, we want to get off at 51st Street!" Nothing happened. I didn't have to look to know that Dapper Man was continuing his slow but steady progress between subway cars. "Keep moving." We rapidly transited cars until we reached the front of the train. Lights flickering inside the car, our train continued its southbound journey all the while a light show of sparks, born of wheel on track contact, danced upon the darkened walls of Manhattan's underground labyrinth. By this time, tears were streaking down Cynthia's cheeks and she was clutching onto Charles' arm. Charles tried to comfort her but empathy was never his strong suit. My eyes rapidly transitioned between the inter-car door and the darkness of the tunnel. My prayers were answered when the bright lighting of the 42nd Street station came into view. A large crowd awaited the coming train. Seeing all the familiar visual cues one might expect on a crowded holiday weekend in the heart of New York had an immediate calming effect. Exiting, we worked our way through the gathered crowd waiting to board the downtown train. Once clear of the mass of humanity, we all looked towards the train to see if Dapper Man would follow us. He was nowhere to be seen. "Well, I was going to suggest we catch 'the 7' over to Times Square but, if you don't mind a little walk, I'm thinking we could all use a little fresh air." There was no disagreement there. On our way, we got to talking about Dapper Man. Although my initial inclination was to avoid the topic, it was pretty clear that we wouldn't be able to consider anything else until we had worked through the bizarre circumstances of our multiple encounters. As bewildered as my friends, I had no great insights to offer. Finally, my "rational mind" checked back in from its coffee break. "I think there's probably a really easy explanation for all of this. There are tons of character players in New York and you're likely to find half a dozen Mickey Mouses or Spider Men on any given day in the City. I'm not really familiar with this Dapper Guy character . . ."

"DAPPER MAN!" my friends simultaneously interjected. I was glad they still found some humor in the situation.

"Yes, I mean Dapper Man character. But, if he's some new social media icon then it makes perfect sense that actors might be playing that role from South Ferry all the way up through Harlem. With that theatrical makeup on, it'd be really hard to tell the actors apart. Right?" I looked at both of my friends and was pleased to see a more relaxed expression come over their faces. I had convinced them. I almost convinced myself. "That guy in the Park was clearly a nut case but the rest of these Dapper Men are probably just out of work actors trying to earn a few bucks from some sponsor." As we were walking down 42nd Street, the famous New York City Public Library came into view.

"Is that the library?" asked Cynthia.

"Let's see now. Ginormous white marble edifice. Imposing lions guarding the stairs. A grand entrance way, bracketed by pillars and the words 'The New York Public Library' etched in stone above the entry. Yes, by George, I think it just may be!" Cynthia punched me on the shoulder.

"Jerk," she said playfully as she smiled. "Let's go look up Dapper Man."

"Are you nuts?"

"No. Now you've got me interested. Let's go see if we can find out what this whole Dapper Man craze is all about."

"Cynth, I'm pretty sure the library closed a couple hours ago." She looked disappointed. I was nearly 100% sure but, to humor

Cynthia, I was willing to take a closer look. As we approached, it became very clear that no one was coming or going. For some reason, I felt the need to state the obvious. "And . . . it's closed."

An old woman, sitting on the library steps, called over to us. She looked somewhat disheveled but I couldn't discern whether she was a homeless woman or merely one of the many eccentrics that gave New York its rare flavor. Her sweet "little old lady voice" was very comforting. We all desperately needed a couple of grandma's homemade cookies and a glass of warm milk.

"I'm so pleased to see young people interested in a library. It seems everyone just wants to walk around looking at their little screens these days."

Cynthia immediately warmed to the old woman. "I love libraries!" There's nothing like the feel of an old book in your hands."

"Now you're talking," said the old woman, with a big grin. That's what I've always said. I used to work as a reference librarian in this very library. The look, the feel, the smell—there's something magical about old books. It looks like you were planning to visit. I'm so sorry. The library closed a couple hours ago."

"Sorry we missed it," said Cynthia. "I've never been to this library but I've heard it's spectacular. You must have all kinds of great stories from your time working in the library. I'm Cynthia, by the way. These are my friends Charles and Patrick. Pat's our local guide here, today. Charles and I are in from California for the long weekend." Charles and I both added in our hellos.

"Charles, eh? That's terrific. I like the old names. It seems like these days everyone wants to jazz up their names or use nicknames. Chaz. Chuckie. C-Rod." The old lady chuckled, sweetly, reflecting upon 'C-Rod'. "I'm Doris. Doris Wiggins. Very pleased to meet you. So, were you here just to look around or were you on a special mission?"

"A special mission," replied Charles. "We met this strange guy in the park and then he showed up a couple more times through the night. A couple folks mentioned that he might be called the Dapper Man so we thought we'd research to see if he was, maybe, advertising some upcoming film or some new product. We were just kind of interested."

The old woman sat quietly for a moment, reflecting. "Ah, S.C. Montague. A darling of a man."

"So, you're familiar with him?" I asked, my interest peaking. "We'd love to hear more if you've got the time."

"Oh, I don't know. There's a lot to tell and I imagine you kids have a hundred places you'd like to visit during your night in the city."

"Oh please," injected Cynthia. "We'd love to hear more. The Big Apple is about stories, after all, not about neon signs and skyscrapers." Her words seemed to inspire the woman.

"Well then, have a seat and buckle up." We all sat on the stone stairs near the woman. She pulled her shawl in closer to keep out the night air as the temperature was quickly dropping.

"S.C. Montague was a well-known performer in his day, right here in New York City. He was quite successful and was adored by theater-goers. But, like many in his day, he watched jealously as the motion picture industry grew and began to get all the attention. Being a star of the stage no longer held the same allure when compared to being a big movie star. They were making silent pictures in those days. He went through a very dark time. He took to the bottle and it only made matters worse. Soon, he found trouble getting work here in New York. He lost his love of life. He lost his fear of God. There are many rumors about what happened next but, cutting out all the ridiculous speculation, I'll just say that fortune took a turn for the better. Much better. He came into a great sum of money. He then received an unsolicited invitation to sign a major motion picture deal for several films with one of Hollywood's largest motion picture studios. Out there, in California, Mr. Montague met and married a beautiful actress, Agnetha Anne Lockborn. She was so stunning that all the Los Angeles papers called her 'The Belle of the West'. This was a very happy time in his life. S.C. Montague rose to national prominence; his clever dance routines held movie goers spellbound from coast to coast and then in Europe and Asia. His career was at its peak. At some point, in the early 1920s, he developed a nagging cough. He visited all the best doctors but none could pinpoint the cause of the affliction nor find a cure. All we know is that his voice became increasingly raspy until, finally, he couldn't speak at all. The only vocalization he was capable of making was a very disturbing screeching noise. The papers said of his voice that it was so hideous it would make babies cry and dogs howl. You should know, the press was never really fair to Mr. Montague."

"Why, what did they have against him?" asked Cynthia.

"Oh, it's hard to know exactly where the falling out occurred. I suspect there was some jealousy of this handsome and talented newcomer from the East Coast who seemed to suddenly rise to fame and glory. Maybe they felt he should have paid his dues for a while and worked his way up the ladder? But, you know, with all his time on stage in New York, he wasn't exactly a rookie. The horrible stories they told. Heartbreaking. Total garbage."

"Like what?" replied Cynthia, completely immersed in the tale.

"Well, there was this one crazy paper that wrote that he had cut a deal with the Devil who offered him the success he dreamed of, on a golden platter, and asked only his soul in exchange. They say the Devil never cuts a fair deal and that it was the Dark One, himself, who reclaimed the voice of S.C. Montague and cursed the poor man with the voice of a demon. Absolute rubbish!" Doris was clearly getting a little upset now. Cynthia, the most empathetic of us, put her hand upon the woman's shoulder and agreed with her that the attacks were ridiculous. Doris took a deep breath and continued.

"In October of 1927, "The Jazz Singer" was released. It was the first major motion picture with synchronized sound and it ushered in a new era in Hollywood. It was no longer good enough to have an expressive face and graceful movements. If you wanted to be a star, you had to have a voice built to steal hearts. I suppose I don't need to tell you what happened next. S.C. Montague's star came plummeting back to earth and his life completely fell apart. Thanks to the bad press, what you kids would probably call "fake news" now, he wasn't even able to find work as a backup dancer in the musicals of the day. His wife left him for one of the up and coming Hollywood glamour guys and S.C., broken of heart and spirit, used his remaining funds to buy a train ticket back to the East Coast. He lived for a while at the Algonquin Hotel, on 44th Street until . . ."

"Where?" said Charles, choking on his words. We all recognized the Algonquin as the place Charles and Cynthia were staying during their visit. Doris didn't seem to hear the question. She was lost in her thoughts and trying to fight back the tears.

"Until 1937. He hung himself in his room. A terrible, terrible tragedy. He was only 37 at the time." What followed was an uncomfortable silence. We all wanted to ask Doris about whether or not she was familiar with any kind of revival or show that might be honoring the legend of S.C. Montague but, given her emotional state, we thought it better just to let it go. About that time, an unusual yellow taxi pulled up. I had only seen cabs like that in old copies of Life Magazine. It was definitely a vintage model . . . maybe late 40s or early 50s. Doris apologized for having to leave but she expressed gratitude for keeping her company while she waited for her ride. The driver came around and opened the door for her and she gave a farewell wave, her white cotton glove highlighted against the night sky, before she slid into the back seat. Nice lady. The cab slipped away into the darkness. Hidden from view, behind the taxi, we now saw the figure of the Dapper Man, standing silent and still across the street.

"Hey, do you want to go talk to that guy?" asked Cynthia. "If anyone can tell us about these mysterious Dapper Men sightings, it's a Dapper Man."

"Fuck, no!" Charles had no desire to learn any more. He was still freaking out about the Algonquin Hotel. "Let's go."

"Times Square?"

"No, Pat. I want to go back to the hotel and I want to catch the first flight back to L.A."

"What?!" said Cynthia, shocked by the sudden change of plans. "We still have another couple days to hang out with Pat. There's a ton of things I want to see."

"We're done, Cynthia. We're going home. If you want to stay, you can hang out with Pat; but I'm outta here."

"You wouldn't mind if I stay?" asked Cynthia.

"Whatever. Knock yourself out." Charles' voice was trembling with fear.

"Okay, follow me." I knew the hotel was within easy walking distance and I also knew that no amount of coaxing was about the change Charles' mind."

We arrived at the hotel and Charles made a direct line to the front desk where he told them he was planning on checking out that evening. The desk attendant explained that the holiday lodging fee was not refundable but the warning had absolutely no impact on my friend. He was a driven man. Cynthia and Charles headed off for the elevator; I decided just to wait in the lobby. I looked around a bit but then curiosity got the better of me. I slowly walked up to the front desk.

"Excuse me. I know this is a strange question but did anyone ever hang themselves in this hotel?" The attendant gave me a strange look.

"You sure know how to start a conversation. Well, it's an old hotel. I couldn't say whether or not anything like that ever happened here."

"If it did, would you tell me?" The attendant considered my question.

"Sir, it's hotel policy not to discuss incidents involving our guests."

"Sooooo . . . no?"

"No. Probably not."

"Probably? Ever hear of a guy called S.C. Montague?" The woman shouted back to the room behind the counter.

"Hank, have you ever heard of a guy called S.C. Montague?" An older gentleman, quite well dressed, slowly emerged from the door.

"You don't have to yell, Charise. I may be old but I can hear just fine. S.C. Montague? The Dapper Man? Yes, I've heard of him."

"Did he hang himself in this hotel?"

"I'm sorry, but it's company policy not to discuss . . ."

I cut the man off before he could finish and completed his words for him "'incidents involving our guests.' I know. Look, this is pretty important and, if I were to maybe donate a substantial tip towards the hotel staff maybe . . ."

This time, it was I who was cut off in mid-sentence. "That would be bribery, wouldn't it? No, I'm sorry, but I can't."

"Look, I'm sorry. This is just really important right now and I can't explain why. I won't tell anyone a thing and, to be honest, I doubt we'll ever see each other again after tonight so," I paused, "what do you say?"

"That was many years ago. All I know is that my predecessor lost two weeks of pay for joking that he only assigned "The Montague Suite" to people he didn't like. The owners didn't take kindly to the remark. First off, it's not a suite. Second, Mr. S.C. Montague was a long-time resident and, although he was rarely seen, he always paid his bills and he always tipped the hotel staff well. Finally, the owners were very disturbed about the whole incident. They were pretty superstitious and felt that Mr. Montague traveled with a dark cloud surrounding him. Frankly, he spooked them and they preferred his name not be mentioned at all. You know how some people are."

"Two weeks of pay? That's a lot. Did they eventually fire him? Is that how you got the job?"

"He was hit by a cab while crossing the street, just a couple blocks down from the hotel. He died in the hospital the next day. That's how I got the job." I swallowed deeply.

"That's awful. I'm sorry to hear that." I held back my follow-up questions long enough to pass for a respectful silence. "The Montague Suite? And which room might that be, Mr.," I squinted as I read his nametag, "Simpson."

Mr. Simpson shook his head in exasperation. "Room 313. But don't you tell anyone I told you." He looked over at the young attendant, "And that goes for you, too."

"Yes, Sir, Mr. Simpson. Silence is silver."

"Golden. Silence is golden." Mr. Simpson retired to the safety of his cave. I returned to the cushy easy chair in the lobby.

Before long, Charles and Cynthia returned. Charles left the bags beside my chair as he and Cynthia went to the desk to check out. In the quiet hotel lobby, I couldn't help but overhear the conversation at the desk."

"Checking out of 313 and, if you wouldn't mind, could you please call me a cab for the airport."

"Absolutely, Sir." The attendant tried to maintain composure but she seemed a bit shaken. She took a quick glance over at me and, no doubt, observed the stunned look upon my face, as well. I debated whether I should say anything about the Montague Suite. I finally concluded that it wouldn't serve any of us to travel down that road. It was best to leave well enough alone.

As a final cherry upon this Twilight Zone evening, it was another strange vintage taxi cab that showed up to take Charles to LaGuardia Airport. I suggested that he request another cab but I had no desire to explain why I was letting my superstition get the best of me . . . so I quickly conceded upon Charles' protest. We said our farewells and then Cynthia and I headed off towards my apartment. I had a little futon in my place that I knew would meet my friend's needs. I was concerned about Charles but looking forward to a little one-on-one time with Cynth, over the next few days.

Cynthia and I did have a wonderful time exploring the city. The weather was pleasantly cool and we got around to see many of the tourist attractions that had been on Cynthia's bucket list. We each sent text messages to Charles and, between stops, tried to call. His failure to respond was a little concerning but we both knew that Charles had a way of "checking off the grid" when he didn't want to be disturbed. I was just hoping that he wasn't upset about Cynthia and me hanging out together for the weekend.

Mid-day, on Monday, I escorted Cynthia back to the airport and saw her off. I missed both my friends. I'd be lying if I said I missed them equally.

Wednesday night, I received what I can only describe as the worst phone call of my life. It was Cynthia and she was in tears. She described how she had visited Charles' apartment on numerous occasions but that he wasn't there. None of their mutual friends had seen him. After a heroic battle with the airline bureaucracy, she finally ascertained that he never actually boarded his flight back to Los Angeles that Saturday night when we parted ways. In short, he had simply disappeared. I tried to comfort Cynthia but I was as much in need of succor as my friend.

Weeks of police investigations followed. The last time anyone had seen Charles was when he got into his taxi at the Algonquin. Cynthia thought that maybe the Dapper Man might have some connection to the disappearance but none of us had any idea how to even bring that up with the authorities. Beyond this, Cynthia was becoming more and more obsessed. She was pouring through any old newspapers archived online to try to find out more about the life of S.C. Montague. As Doris had warned us, many of the papers were not kind. One trashy rag even called him Satan's Child Montague. Beyond the litany of terrible accusations, Cynthia desperately tried to sort out fact from fiction. Occasionally, she'd call me to report her latest findings. In truth, I had heard about all I wanted to hear on the topic. She did gain my full attention when she ran through Mr. Montague's family tree.

"Pat, you remember the woman we met at the library?"

"Right. I don't recall her name but she sure seemed like an expert on the Dapper Man."

"So, when S.C. Montague married Agnetha Anne Lockborn, you know, the Belle of the West, they had two daughters—Gladys and

Patience. Gladys and Patience remained with Agnetha in California. Eventually, Patience came east, to New York. Her father had already passed away by that time but she attempted, briefly, to establish a career on Broadway. Unfortunately, she wasn't finding enough work to pay the bills. So . . ."

"Where is this going, Cynth?"

"Just hear me out. So, she marries this cello player with the New York Philharmonic and they have a couple kids—a boy and a girl. The girl gets married to Charles Wiggins, a banker. The oldest daughter from that wedding is named Doris. Doris Wiggins!"

"Doris Wiggins?"

"Yes, Doris Wiggins! That was the name of the old lady we met on the stairs at the library."

"So, Cynth, you think we were talking to the granddaughter of S.C. Montague?" The line was silent for a bit.

"Okay. So, I did. But then I did some more research. Doris Wiggins was, in fact, a librarian with the New York Public Library. She tried to restore her grandfather's reputation as best she could but the public had moved on and nobody gave the matter much mind."

"My turn," I said, impatient to get to the point. "So, let me guess, she decided to create a Broadway play called 'Three Cheers for S.C.' to honor her grandfather and it's due to open next week and a dozen Dapper Men are running around the City to advertise the upcoming shows?" The line was silent.

"Pat, Doris Wiggins died in 1987."

"Okay. Look, Cynth, I want you to let this thing go. It isn't doing you any good to obsess about this. I miss Charles, too. I know how close you were and I can only imagine the pain you're going through but this is not helpful. There are no ghosts sitting on the steps of the New York Public Library and no tap-dancing demons entertaining visitors in Central Park. We saw some weird stuff during your visit but that's all it was—weird stuff. The world is full of weird things and weird people and yet we continue on our journeys and make the best of it." I went on and on and on. Sometimes, I felt like I was working as hard to convince myself as I was to convince Cynthia. Finally, she conceded, and made a kissing sound through the phone to show her affection.

"Love ya, Pat."

"Love ya, back, Cynth."

I waited for Cynthia to hang up first. I didn't want to risk cutting her off if she had anything more to say. After a lengthy pause, she ended the call.

At this point, I just really needed to clear my head. Although I had given a wide berth to Central Park since the Dapper Man incident, I thought it might be beneficial to confront my silly fears and take a little stroll through the park before all the holiday crowds arrived for the Thanksgiving experience in New York City. I was just praying to God that they didn't fly a Dapper Man balloon in the Macy's Thanksgiving Day Parade this year.

Although it was quite cool, the park was very inviting and I derived a strange pleasure from kicking at the small piles of dead leaves I encountered as I wandered the grounds. I emerged from the woods near where we first saw the Dapper Man. I stopped dead in my tracks. There he was! Dancing with renewed vigor and entertaining the small pre-holiday crowd that had gathered to admire his footwork. Just turn and go. Just turn and go. I swayed back and forth as my fear drove me one way and my curiosity beckoned me towards the familiar stage. I squinted, trying to make out the features of the Dapper Man's face. My heart was gripped with pure terror as the features came into focus. It was Charles! I began to run towards him but my legs locked up and I fell. I quickly returned to my feet and continued running as I yelled "Charles! Charles! It's me, Pat!" The dancer continued. I ran up to him and grabbed him by both shoulders. "Charles! What the Hell! What in God's name are you doing here?! Everyone thinks you're dead!" The dancer just looked at me with hollow, expressionless, eyes. I know I was not mistaken. There was no doubt that this was Charles. I spoke again, my voice frantic, "Charles, what's happened to you, man?" The crowd grew very unsettled and I started to gain their ire.

"Hey, Dude, leave the Dapper Man alone. Let him do his dance," shouted a rather burly looking fellow who appeared to be a construction worker on break. The sentiment was echoed by a chorus of assorted pleas to get out of the way and stop ruining the performance.

I took one last, long, look into the familiar face. And then I realized . . . this was no longer Charles. Any part of the friend I once knew was long gone from the shell of humanity that danced before the gleeful crowd of spectators. The Dapper Man looked right through me, his face void of any expression. I slowly backed away. I just stood there and watched the dance. He was quite good. Very good, to be precise. I looked into my wallet to see if I had any money to offer as a tip. All I had was two twenty-dollar bills. I pulled them both out and left them in a little tin box next to the performer. Dapper Man tipped his hat, ever so slightly, acknowledging the donation. I turned and walked away. A couple beer guzzling ruffians passed by me, as I walked. They were singing a mocking version of Elton John's "Tiny Dancer" and joking about beating the heck out of the dancing performer.

I stopped and turned around. "Hey!Assholes!" That got their attention. They stopped abruptly and looked at me, assessing whether I was someone they wanted to mess with or not. I stood silently for a bit. I hadn't really thought through my plan. Finally, I said the only thing that came to mind, the only piece of advice I wish Charles, Cynthia, and I had received sooner than we did. In my loudest voice I shouted "DON'T FUCK WITH DAPPER MAN!" And then I walked away.

About David Lange

Colonel David Lange was born and grew up on Long Island, New York. A graduate of the United States Air Force Academy, he served for 30 years as an Active Duty officer in the United States Air Force before retiring in 2018. Colonel Lange is a decorated combat veteran, and flew numerous combat, combat support, and humanitarian relief missions during his career. He was awarded the prestigious Institute of Navigation Superior Achievement Award in recognition of his life-long accomplishments as a practicing navigator. David loves sharing stories of hope and inspiration and, in 2020, he published his memoir, "Quest: My Journey Through La Mancha."

Also by David Lange

Quest: My Journey Through La Mancha

Connect with David Lange

www.davidlangequest.com

PART V

The Beauty Within - Stories of Spirituality, Faith, and Love

In this edition of The Red Penguin Collection, join us as we embark on a spiritual journey that transcends the realm of the everyday. Within these pages, prepare yourself to be moved by the beautiful words that make up an anthology of poetry, prose, and prayers centered around the faith that we carry with us as we go about our lives. As we fall deeper into harmony with our inner beings, so must we read of the stories of others. "The Beauty Within" lies ahead.

1

The Children's Moment

LINDA TROTT DICKMAN

For all the beautiful brothers, including mine

There at the foot

of the minister,

listening for the story, she sat,

draped in black velvet

crème organza, gold sparkles.

Her long hair gathered in a crushed curl

of red flowing down her back.

She realized…her dress was unzipped.

She simply turned to her brother

and mouthed "Please? Zip me?"

No words. A quizzical look, then

his awkward hands found the zipper

and coaxed it up the track.

Peace on Earth.

About Linda Trott Dickman

Linda Trott Dickman has been writing poetry since her first sleep-away camp experience when she was ten years old. Linda is the author of Robes, The Air That I Breathe and Road Trip. Linda's poetry has been published on-line, in Pratik Journal and in several anthologies. She is the current coordinator of poetry for the Northport Arts Coalition (Northport, NY.), has taught poetry to children for over 35 years and leads a poetry workshop for adults at Samantha's Li'l Bit O' Heaven coffee house in East Northport, NY.

Also by Linda Trott Dickman

Robes

The Air That I Breathe

Road Trip

Connect with Linda Trott Dickman

Facebook - Linda Trott Dickman

Blog - https://libearyn.wordpress.com/

2

New Orleans

ELAINE DONADIO

The Big Easy—so edgy,
rolls its soulful eyes.
Jesus and voodoo.
Parties and prayer.
Celebrate life.
Honor death.
Live oaks embrace the sky.
Visitors walk in the shadow of Christ.
Streets—so hot.
Jazz—so cool.
Consonance. Dissonance. Improvisation.
Wail that trumpet.
Tickle those ivories.
Pluck that banjo.
Trill that horn.
Pound those skins.
Legato. Staccato.
Sway. Swing, Sashay.
Let the good times roll.

Faithless levees—so sad,
once protected by alluvial soil,
conspired with the shameless
to impel hapless souls
submerged beneath the coursing torrents
to an audience with
the Lord Jesus Christ.
Corralled. Abandoned. Dispersed.

Ghosts of tortured souls—so lamentable.
Stalking. Jumping. Trailing.
Victims of slavery, crime, disease,
oppressive heat and humidity,
natural disasters and wartime occupation.
They cry out in pain and fear.
Tortured. Burned. Mistreated.
Medical and carnival experiments,
limbs and body parts exchanged.
Pleas ignored.
Prayers unanswered.
Cities of the Dead—so esteemed,
rise up to give shelter.
Wall vaults, a year and a day prelude to family tombs,
crypts and mausoleums
in a gumbo that blends
cultures, races, and social strata,
simmered and stirred by
common experiences in life
and shared spaces in death,
served over yellow mums
to welcome protection of the saints.
Laissez les bons temps rouler—so joyful.
Purple for justice.
Green for faith.

Gold for power.
Baby Jesus nestled in the womb of the
Twelfth Night King Cake.
Fat Tuesday, Mardi Gras,
begins the fasting season of Lent.
Costumes. Masks. Gemstones.
Plumes. Feathers.
"Throw me something."
Beads. Doubloons. Trinkets.
Get down.
Positively.
Absolutely.
Yeah.

About Elaine Donadio

Author. Poet. Blogger. Book reviewer. Reading Specialist at New York City Schools, Elaine Donadio's characters reflect the urban lifestyle. She writes about what she loves, using well-researched facts to feed your head, your heart and your soul. She's concerned about the effects of human carelessness on the world in which we live. Learning is the point but better viewed through experiences that communicate awe as the world unfolds its secrets. Readers can laugh and learn at the same time.

Study guides in alignment with state standards for science, social studies, and literacy are available at elainedonadio.com.

Also by Elaine Donadio

The Montgomery School Kids Series

The Science Project

The Ocean's Way

Who Do Voodoo?

March of the Blue Moon

Other Books

The Ocean's Way Poetry Companion

Sojourn Into The Night—A Memoir of the Peruvian Rainforest

Short Stories

"Shape Shifters of the Shinulaktup" Red Penguin Press (2020) Anthology: *I Can't Find My Flashlight*

Connect with Elaine Donadio

https://elainedonadiowrites.wordpress.com/

www.facebook.com/ElaineWritesNow

http://twitter.com/ElaineDonadio1

www.linkedin.com/in/ElaineDonadio

3

A Collection of Poems

JENNA ZEIHEN

God

A lavender mind wakes thousands, it's a blur.

Reds, blues, bodies, taking you in nightmares and in dreams.

Gates close.

I can see waves with purple angels -what faith loves tonight.

The moon said, "no."

Singing through time, what holds your night?

Invading the quiet when eyes light the sky.

You weren't born just to die–

I see God in your eyes.

What I'll find

Maybe, beneath which is seen in you,

Room for present

Lasting,

sky is what I'll find.

If my soul were free, what would she look like?

Would she look like me?

Lightly touching, hands,

Eyes meet across the room.

I am closest to God when I'm near you.

You

You have swam through oceans no one else will ever know,

You have held the hands of more people than we will ever know,

You have left a mark on every person that has ever met you.

a light sparkles bright in every heart you've ever touched–

the human form of sunlight,

the earthly kind of heaven,

You are grace and power

wrapped in more than anyone could ever hope to be,

or see,

or know,

or love

so thank you, because
You have saved my life,
more than i've ever said
or realized.
You have stood through the storm
and the rain
and have lost–
You have lost pieces of what feels like
your heart and soul
and maybe your whole being.

but You are found in this room;
You are found every time i smile
because You have brought me here.
You are found every time i get up in the morning
because You have brought me here.
You are found every time i see the sun set
because You have brought me here.
You are every reason God is real
and life is good
and loss is finding something good again.

please know that the mountains You cross are worth more than anything i could ever give to You in return, but

i hope this late night letter

reminds You now and then,

how much one year can change a person,

and how much your love has the true power to change,

and heal,

and make beautiful light out of nothing at all.

and–

when you're feeling alone,

or missing those who are gone,

or missing how things used to be–

remember the us we were a year ago,

and remember how proud i am

of Us for who we are

now.

always and always and always.

About Jenna Lee Jane Zeihen

Jenna is currently studying Communication and Gender Studies at Carthage College, loves to write, vlog, and make digital artwork. She is an advocate for the chronic illness and Mast Cell Disease community, and hopes to continue growing, and loving, and writing on her journey!

Connect with Jenna Lee Jane Zeihen

instagram.com/jennaleejane

https://www.youtube.com/channel/UC2fFiaUt4ucf9-JifraZuTw

4

Letter to God

JACQUELINE BOTTENBLEY

As I look out upon your vast wonders of beauty and tranquility, I wonder why it can't all be like this. You are so powerful and still you choose to give us free will. How unselfish and loving you are, giving us freedom, knowing what we will do to the beauty we have created. How hurt you must be, though you will never reveal your pain.

I look at the beauty of water, which I truly enjoy. I plunge into freedom as it washes away the burdens of the world. A peace and serenity engulf me and there is nothing else.

I see the beauty of the trees, the oxygen they give, that we absorb every minute of everyday, and yet don't appreciate. We take for granted the breath of life as if it is owed to us, never thanking you for each breath we take, never appreciating and enjoying the beauty of the trees that sustain our very life.

I hear the murmur of the waves and wonder, are you speaking to me, or is it the creatures of the sea rejoicing in song? Is it a conversation of the sea? Is it a chorus of the creatures of sea and air chiming in succession for our enjoyment? A chorus of song we are too busy to hear. Each animal rejoices with a different tune. How wonderful you are. Your creativity is endless. Humanity rejoices in different languages, yet you give us the wisdom, knowledge, and desire to understand one another. You wish for all to be united as one, yet human frailty inhibits us.

The vastness of the blue sky I seem to get lost in. I yearn to be apart, above the world, looking down on the panorama of creation.

The night sky and its stars are your watchful eyes, guiding us through the valley of the dark. The haze of humanity dims our view to the soul of the sky. Now we realize what we have missed and yearn to reach out to you. We desire that you watch us and guide us. Teach us patience and open our eyes, minds, and hearts so that we can absorb you and be absorbed by you.

About Jacqueline Bottenbley

A teacher for 23 years. I am an avid reader. Love dancing, arts and crafts.

Also by Jacqueline Bottenbley

Realiteen from The Red Penguin Collection

Connect with Jacqueline Bottenbley

Facebook, linked in. Alignable Jacqueline Bottenbley

5

Dance of Spirits

BRIANNA WITTE

I slowly moved away from the bonfire, my moccasins sliding deep into the freezing, wet snow. The bitter cold wind clawed at my exposed face and weakened the flame on the torch I held.

I exited the large cave, the soft glow of the moon hitting my eyes. I followed the mountain pass, my gloved hand running against the hard, frozen, rocky ledge. Slowly, the looming mountain dissipated, leaving me staring out into the snow covered valley below.

The frozen lake spread out for miles; the thick ice glimmering in the moonlight. The Winter breeze blew the soft snow into the air, sending it flying over the beautiful valley. In the distance, the large, furry buffalo grazed; their thick noses digging for plants under the deep snow. Three young calves ran through the snow, their heavy hooves kicking up the slush around the lake's edge.

As I watched the calves, both sadness and anger crept upon me. I could hear it still. The thunderous sound of the herd of buffalo running. The shouts of my fellow Kaska First Nations brethren as they targeted a small, lone calf. And the sound of the mother buffalo running at my brother, her thick, sharp horns aimed to kill.

Tears slid down my shivering face, my skin tingling as the cold merged with my warm, wet tears. My brother. My best friend. The only person who truly understood me now lay silent and unmoving under a thick wall of ice, his body becoming one with the river; one of the many flowing veins of this land.

Watching the buffalo run freely and peacefully filled me with anger. I wanted to throw my hunting spear at them. Throw my pain. I had never felt so alone before. Never felt this thick wall of ice building around my heart.

Disappointment rushed through me. I was going back to our tribe empty handed and with one less person. Sure, another group of healthy, strong young men would go out and search for food. However, in the meantime our tribe would be going hungry. They were dependent on us and we had let them down. One less man meant one less hunter to find food; one less person to feed our people during the cold, frozen season.

It should be me decaying into the ground. I froze when I saw the large, mother buffalo charging. I froze and he died to protect me. I was just a young boy out on his first hunt while my brother was one of our best hunters and warriors. It should have been me.

A glimmering light glistened in the corner of my eye. Wiping the tears from my face, I looked up towards the stars. A colourful spectacle of light appeared before me, lighting up the night sky.

For a second, it felt like all of the air was stripped from my lungs. My eyes went wide in astonishment. I couldn't believe the beautiful phenomenon laid out before me.

The Northern Lights spread out for miles with no end in sight. The lake's dark, ice-coated surface reflected the stunning aura, making the valley look like it had been transported to a mystical realm.

A loud sob escaped my cold lips. He slowly appeared in the glimmering lights; his thin, angular face and strong arms unmistakable. I knew it was him the moment I saw him. My brother looked down on me from the lights; his soul merged with the sky.

In that moment, the ice that had formed around my heart began to melt. The pain and sadness that overcame me was lifted from my shoulders, freeing my soul from the grief that held me down. Looking into my brother's eyes, I knew he was at peace and, in turn, I could be, too. Although he was gone, my brother was all around me. In the air, in the water, in the land and, of course, in me. I was not alone; I never was. He will always be with me.

With my heart released from the darkness swirling within, my brother's soul turned away, merging back into the Lights.

Up between the stars, our loved ones lived; their bodies gone but souls alive. They celebrate life. Celebrate death. Celebrate our existence.

The Northern Lights are a dance of spirits; a sign that no one is ever really gone.

About Brianna Witte

As a writer from Ontario, Canada, Brianna has a passion for spinning tales of adventure and fantasy. She enjoys taking readers on a ride through the realm of fiction by weaving magical and mystical stories that materialize from her wildly creative dreams and vivid imagination.

Brianna is an active member of the Writers Community of Durham Region. She had received a commendation for her short story, The Hunt, in the 2019 Author of Tomorrow Award by the Wilbur and Niso Smith Foundation. To date, Brianna has had many short stories published in various anthologies.

On December 1, 2019, Brianna released her first book, Witches and Vampires, published by Atmosphere Press. Witches and Vampires is also a proud winner of the 2020 Canada Book Awards.

Also by Brianna Witte

Witches and Vampires

(Novella - published December 2019)

Connect with Brianna Witte

https://www.facebook.com/BriannaWitteAuthor/

https://www.instagram.com/briannawitteauthor/

PART VI

The Moments

The Moments is an anthology of pieces from ***The Red Penguin Collection*** that celebrate the many instances of life most worthy of celebration.

For when you are struggling, when the nights seem to last forever, when you lay in bed and cannot find the strength within you to crawl off of the mountain of cushions that have built up over weeks of living in the same spot, this is for you.

Through the works of these amazing and wildly different voices, I hope that such a book offers as much hope to you as working on such projects has given me.

1

Christmas Kindness

SKYE BALANTYNE

The air was crisp and I shivered as I wrapped my jacket tighter around my shoulders and my breath puffed out in front of me, making me look like a dragon. Any day now, the kids would be out for their Christmas break. The spirit of Christmas and giving was in the air, and I could feel it seeping into my bones with every step I made toward my work.

I stepped inside and was assaulted with another donation. Food, clothes, toys, and all manner of products filled the conference room, spilling out into the hallways and into the lobby. There was hardly enough space for us to walk around in, let alone house any more donations. It was a humbling sight, realizing how many people cared and gave during the holiday season.

I was just in the middle of sorting out the gifts–trying to make sure every child got something to unwrap–when the sound of the doorbell jerked me out of my work. I got to my feet and opened the door. In front of me was a mom with her little girl.

"I bought this toy," the little girl said without preamble, practically pushing the doll at me to take, "I thought maybe another little girl might like to have it."

I took the doll out of the little girl's hand with a smile. It never ceased to amaze me how giving children could really be–especially around the holidays. I never saw someone more excited about dropping off a donation than a child at Christmas time. Yet, no matter how many times I saw it, it never ceased to melt my heart and remind me of the goodness in people. It reminded me why I did what I did.

"She paid for it using her own money too," the mother added as I held the doll close, "She wanted to make sure other little kids had Christmas, too."

I could feel the tears pricking my eyes as I held the doll even closer and my heart melted into a puddle. As they left, I couldn't help thinking about the child who would get the doll this girl had just delivered. I knew just the child. I knew how much she would LOVE it. I wished I would be able to see her face when she opened the gift, but it would be enough to be able to know she had gotten the perfect gift for Christmas, thanks to the love of a stranger–a little girl not much older than her.

The Christmas spirit continued to flow through us and the shelter. People continued to drop off donations and the members of staff were hard at work, wrapping up presents for our residents and their children.

"Oh hey," one of our residents said as she pulled out a bag of presents for her, "They got me something, too."

You could tell from her voice that she hadn't been expecting it. She hadn't thought anyone would give her anything for Christmas. She had been so involved in making sure her child would still have a magical Christmas that she had totally forgotten about herself and had thought others had, too.

I don't remember which of us moved first–me or my coworker–but together we raced to her side and grabbed the bag out of her hands. The presents weren't wrapped. She shouldn't be in charge of wrapping her own presents, and she should have something to unwrap with her child on Christmas morning.

That evening, the group of residents gathered in our common areas and wrapped presents for their children. While they worked on making sure their children had the perfect Christmas, the next morning, my coworker and I were hard at work making sure that the adults, too, had a perfect Christmas. We wrapped gifts, hiding behind our desks and whispering conspiratorially as we laughed when residents came up to us to ask for tape or scissors.

We were like giddy children, unable to contain our excitement for Christmas and the shocked and happy looks that we knew would be on their faces as we placed the gifts under the tree so they could be unwrapped the next morning. They were far from perfect. A child could have probably done a better job with the wrapping than we had been able to do, but, with each mistake and mess up, we convinced ourselves that it was the thought that counted, and not how pretty our work was.

"Hey, I think we're doing pretty good, given the space we have available to work with," my coworker said when I made a comment on how terrible my wrapping job had been.

Sure, I would go with that. Lack of wrapping space was TOTALLY the only reason the presents looked like a monkey had tried to wrap them while getting trampled by a herd of elephants going by. It had nothing to do with the fact that I had absolutely no idea how to wrap a present and make it look decent, even if I had all the room in the world to do so.

"Merry Christmas!" my coworker said as we finally put the finishing touches on the gifts. She was supposed to go home hours ago, but she had been too caught up in the excitement of wrapping presents to actually leave when she was supposed to, and I hadn't pushed it. I hadn't minded the help.

"Merry Christmas!" I said, giving her a hug as I watched her leave to be with her family come morning.

With the presents all wrapped, at least on our end, there was nothing to do but to wait for the residents to finish wrapping all their presents as well and head to their rooms for the night.

I knew I could technically tell them all it was time for them to go to bed. It was, after all, nearly two in the morning at that point, but it was Christmas, and they hadn't finished wrapping presents yet, so I didn't have the heart to send them to bed quite yet. I would let them finish their last touches to make the day as special as they could. I could wait........

As time dragged on, and the morning sun was fast approaching, I found myself watching the residents more and more impatiently, waiting for them to finish and head to their rooms so that I could do what I needed to do.

It seemed like it took them ages to finish up, but, finally, one by one each of the residents filed back to their own rooms and closed their doors. The living room was empty! It was my turn to shine. I slipped back to their tree, ready to be loaded with presents. I wished I had dressed up a bit–maybe put on a Santa suit or an elf costume, or at the very least a Santa hat–but no, I hadn't done any of that. Too late now. I had to go with what I had. It wasn't as if anyone was going to see me anyway, that was the whole point.

I took each present–as pathetically wrapped as they were–and placed them underneath the Christmas tree with the presents the residents had just finished wrapping. There were more presents than I thought, and most of them didn't end up fitting underneath the tree. When all the presents were laid out there in the living room, I stepped back and examined my work.

Sure, the presents weren't stacked neatly, and most of the presents looked like a two year old had been allowed to wrap them unsupervised, and there was no way that it was going to make any Christmas cards or win any awards for prettiest Christmas tree, but all the presents were there and I couldn't have felt more proud of the accomplishment.

Satisfied, I made my way back to my desk and turned on some Christmas music to ring in the Christmas morning the right way. It didn't seem like I had been up there more than a few minutes before I could hear the sounds of children waking up.

"Santa came! Santa came!" the kids shouted as they raced into the living room and saw all the presents under, around, and near the tree.

I watched the looks on the adults' faces as the number of presents seemed to almost double in a few short hours.

"This one is for you mama," a child said, handing a present to their mother.

I watched their faces. This was the best part. Her face lit up, and I could see a smile spread across as she held the present in her hand. I could see tears forming in her eyes. Tears of happiness, of joy, of hope.

Although it was more tape than wrapping paper, and what little wrapping paper there was looked more like trash than a present, it was a gift–a gift for her and her alone. That little present meant that she hadn't been forgotten about. That present meant that, no matter what was going on in her life at that moment, no matter what had brought her to us in the first place, she hadn't been forgotten about. She wasn't alone. She was loved. People who didn't even know her had taken the time to buy something so that she was able to have a Merry Christmas as well.

My heart once again melted. As I watched our residents cry their tears, I felt my tears start pricking my eyes as well as my heart flooded with love and peace. It didn't matter what was in the present. It didn't matter that it was terribly wrapped, it didn't even have to be wrapped at all. That little gift, no matter how small, meant the world to them, because it proved to them that there was goodness in the world, there was love. It gave them hope, and that was the greatest gift in the world.

As their tears fell down their cheeks, I felt my own eyes begin to prick as my heart filled up and flooded out through my eyes. It was indeed a precious sight to behold. In that small moment of time, I was able to truly see what the magic of Christmas was all about, and I quietly gave a small voice of thanks to the kindness of strangers–the people who chose to donate so that other people were able to have the same joy on Christmas morning as they would. I was filled with the love these people had for strangers–people they may never even see and yet chose to help. It was enough to make me a little sad when it was time for me to go home and celebrate Christmas with my own family.

In that short moment of time I felt the true magic of Christmas. I was allowed to see just how beautiful it could be. That first Christmas I was able to see what Christmas was truly all about and I came to realize that the real and most important moments in our lives aren't the big ones, after all.

Life is about the little moments. That small act of kindness, though it may not have changed a life, brightened a day. That small moment of joy when your child or pet comes running up to you to greet you after a long, hard day. The smell of brownies being baked. Spending time with loved ones. The time when connections are made and life is a little brighter. These gifts of life do not always come in the shiny wrapping paper and big bows; sometimes the most precious moments a life can have come in small packages that are more tape than wrapping paper, with wrapping paper that looks like it belongs in a trash bin rather than on a present. These are the simple moments that mean the most.

About Skye Ballentyne

Skye Ballantyne has always had the desire to write from a young age. She had stories that she just had to get down onto paper; stories that refused to be silent. They needed to be shared with the world. As she grew, she desired to write a story that would make people feel the same way she did when she read some of her favorite books. She took to writing and hasn't looked back since.

Skye also enjoys helping people and bringing awareness to different social causes to help make this world a better place to live in, one with more love and acceptance.

Skye has a blog where she writes on a writing prompt each day

Also by Sky Ballantyne

The Worlds In The Woods Series (5 Book series)

Privacy Denied

Connect with Skye Ballantyne

https://www.facebook.com/skye.ballantyne.7

https://www.instagram.com/skyeswriting/

https://www.skyeballantyne.com/

https://scatteredthinker.weebly.com/

https://www.amazon.com/Skye-Ballantyne/e/B086Z4BHLJ?ref_=dbs_p_pbk_r00_abau_000000

2

Bonding with Lifers

CHRISTINA HOAG

The students start lining up at the fence when they see me walking down to the block of classrooms that lies just outside the prison yard. They have to be on a list to leave the maximum-security cell blocks and yard, where they're confined day in and day out, and then patted down by an officer. Once they're through the gate, they rush to the classroom for my writer's workshop class. The first thing they do is shake my hand. They don't get a lot of physical contact with people.

They are lifers at California State Prison-Los Angeles County. Most are LWOPs, sentenced for murder to life without possibility of parole. As many of the lifers note, there's a "P" missing in the LWOP acronym, the P of possibility. Others are sentenced to such heavy time--fifty, sixty, seventy years--that it's equivalent to LWOP. It's not officially the death penalty but it has the same outcome. They will die in prison. The men call their fate simply "life without," or more wryly, "toe-tag parole," referring to the practice in morgues of placing identification tags on the big toes of cadavers.

"The only way I'm leaving here is in a box," one man says in a matter-of-fact tone.

They always thank me for making the ninety-mile trek from Los Angeles into Southern California's wind-whipped high desert. As I drive up the freeway, the housing tracts and big-box stores give way to a jagged, dun-colored landscape of rocks and mountains. It seems to symbolize the harsh and barren isolation in which prisoners live.

For the majority of them, I am one of few people from the outside they see regularly other than prison staff. Most men have been incarcerated since adolescence or young adulthood, the high-risk age for committing crimes. The criminal justice system offers little redemption for the terrible mistakes of youth. Many, if not most, of the guys have matured into adulthood in prison but they will have no second chance to demonstrate their maturity to anyone but themselves.

Most have little in the way of contact with their families, some none at all. Their perpetual sentences mean loved ones gradually turn two-dimensional, frozen into the folds of fading memory and old photos. Families find keeping in touch over decades a burden. Collecting phone calls and care packages is expensive. The remote location of prisons makes visits few and far between. Writing old-fashioned letters, a lifeline for prisoners, is an extra chore. Some families simply cut off contact out of shame of their incarcerated relative.

In this warehouse of shipwrecked souls, all I can do is encourage the men to write. Writing offers them a chance to build self-esteem and a sense of achievement, to make lives crashed by disastrous choices worthy, to redefine their existence as men not inmate numbers. It provides an outlet for introspection and reflection on how they ended up surrounded by coils of razor wire, and a release of the shame and guilt they carry. I remind them they need only a pencil and a piece of paper to escape the fences and the prison of judgment, both their own and society's. They drink the words. Motivation is a rare commodity in this place of small hope and purposeless existence.

After a year, I've bonded with the class. Before the lesson begins, we chitchat about what we've all been doing. I'm always struck how they have made their lives in prison. It's their home. One guy shows me a gap in his mouth where he had a tooth out. Another tells me he's become a grandfather. I ask about a back problem, progress on an appeal. They relish the interest in their lives. Then one man sticks his hand up and asks what I have learned from "a bunch of convicts." The class is quiet, waiting to hear my answer. Their eyes trained on me, I grope for something eloquent to say. I don't want to say anything trite or something that would hurt their feelings, then much to my relief, I find the words.

Life is not about the accomplishments and material success that we so fervently chase. It's about slivers of interaction with others that reveal we share the same precarious journey underneath the superficial characteristics of gender, race, background and circumstance. It's about the impact that we can make on others' lives through connection. There is no price to be placed on uplifting one another by offering hope, friendship, compassion even in fleeting snatches.

Moments are all we have in the prison. A litany of picayune, infantilizing rules circumscribes time and movement so tightly that personal exchanges are necessarily compressed. Precisely because of the limitations, they are all the more cherished. A mutual laugh or a flash of a smile, the arch of an eyebrow or an eye-roll, any of which may last merely a split-second, becomes a tiny treasure of connection.

There are also monumental moments where the truth that each of us is an interwoven thread in this tapestry called the human condition is laid bare.

After class one day, one of the men pulls me aside in the hallway. In a low rumbling drawl, he tells me he's afraid I'll think badly of him when I read his writing about his past. I am so moved that he's worried about my approval, I feel a pang in my chest. I realize that even though he has done awful things, he wants to be seen as more than the worst deed he's ever done. We all want approval from others, to be seen in a clement light, to not be judged, him no less than me.

Another day before class, I'm chatting to a sculptor in the art room, a couple doors down from my classroom. Full of paintings, drawings and sculptures, the art room is an oasis of color in the prison, which is full of drab institutional greys and beiges. Except for the artists' uniform clothing – prison blue pants and shirts, it feels like it could be an art room in any school. For some reason, I mention that my apartment was burglarized years ago when I was a college student. To my surprise, the sculptor slaps his palm to his heart. "That really hurts me right here. I used to break into houses when I was a kid. I'm really sorry that happened to you."

Another artist is sitting nearby. "Dude, you're exercising empathy," he informs him.

The sculptor's face shines like a baby fresh out of a bath. "Yeah, man, I'm exercising empathy!"

I can't help but laugh at his sheer delight at being able to show empathy, something that he's had to learn through classes in prison. It is a moment of success for him.

Writers use words to express our deepest selves, and I share many moving moments with the men when I am alone with their pages, handwritten in pen or pencil. A man soon to be paroled after nearly three decades of incarceration writes of his fear of foundering in the outside world. Incarcerated since the age of nineteen, he knows little about navigating life beyond the razor wire. The outside world seems big, fast-paced and full of things he's never done before, from holding a baby to holding a job. He's especially anxious about relating to women after living in a hypermasculine world for decades. Who has lived a life free of failure or the fear of being unable to find love? We've all been there.

I unfold another sheaf of papers. One of the men has decided to confront the painful legacy of a boyhood sexual assault he endured more than thirty years ago. Printed at the top of the page, he writes, "Please don't tell anyone about this." I choke up. I'm honored that he has trusted me to reveal this secret to and proud of his courage. We all keep painful secrets.

As a class, we share many moments. The men read aloud essays about their long-ago lives. Some relate the circumstances that steered them into this bastion of banishment. Their stories have a lot of common threads, obstacles from early ages that would have made it hard for them not to land in prison. Many grew up without fathers, some never even met them. One was abandoned as a newborn in a hospital. Another was raised by a crack-addicted mother. One was a runaway living on the streets at age twelve, but he writes of a fond memory, of when he was a little boy, riding in a car with his father pumping the brakes in time to James Brown on the radio. He smiles as he reads his piece and we all feel happy with him. A Vietnam combat veteran relates how he would find his dad, a violent alcoholic, at the curb and call his Alcoholics Anonymous sponsor in futile attempts to save him from himself. "I don't know why I loved my father, but I did," he wrote.

"All children desperately want to love their parents even when they don't love us back," I tell the class. Heads nod. We all carry that innocent desire within us forever.

I am beckoned outside one day by one of the men. His eyes glisten, and I wonder what's coming. "I know I've said that I'm innocent, but I decided I have to tell the truth," he says quietly. "I killed my wife. I just wanted you to know."

His sudden confession takes me aback, although I'm not surprised. I've never really believed his story. Still, what on earth do you say to someone who confesses to murdering a wife with whom he had a baby? I certainly can't condone the act, nor lying about it for more than thirty years, but then the answer comes to me. I thank him for trusting me enough to tell me, for his bravery in voicing the truth. Reassured, he thanks me for accepting him. Everyone has done things they're ashamed of, has told lies in an effort to avoid blame or generate sympathy. We share a moment of acknowledgment in the frailty and imperfection of being human.

As I drive home after the class, I am always overwhelmed with the sense of "there but for the grace of God go I," of the total random nature of the accident of birth that sets the foundation for our personal choices and our life outcomes. What have I learned from a bunch of convicts? That no matter who we are, we are all human beings.

About Christina Hoag

Christina Hoag is the author of two novels Girl on the Brink, named to Suspense Magazine's Best YA list, and Skin of Tattoos, Silver Falchion Award finalist. She also co-authored the nonfiction book Peace in the Hood: Working with Gang Members to End the Violence. A former journalist, she reported from Latin America for Time, Financial Times, New York Times and other media. Her short stories and essays have been published in numerous literary journals. She recently won Honorable Mentions for essay and short story in the International Human Rights Arts Festival Literary Awards 2020.

Also by Christina Hoag

Skin of Tattoos

Girl on the Brink

Nonfiction

Peace in the Hood: Working with Gang Members to End the Violence

Connect with Christina Hoag

https://www.christinahoag.com

https://facebook.com/ChristinaHoagAuthor

https://twitter.com/ChristinaHoag

https://www.instagram.com/ChristinaHoagAuthor

3

Touched by Rapture

JIM TRITTEN

June 15th, 2019, Corrales, New Mexico. I turned my computer on, and after the screen settled down, I looked at a posting on Facebook. It was from an organization I had never heard of–No Barriers, USA. They were advertising openings for a nine-day Warrior expedition to Big Bend National Park in Texas. I scrolled down the page and saw it was open to veterans with a service-connected disability. The following motto permeated their web site: "What's within you is stronger than what's in the way." I watched a video about one of their co-founders, Eric Weihenmayer. Blind since his teenage years, Eric climbed Mount Everest. I thought, if he could do that, I could do this. I filled out the online application. After all, I had been a Navy carrier pilot and was used to meeting challenges on the fly.

On Saturday, October 5th, I joined nine other veterans and five leaders in Midland, Texas, for the most physically challenging experience of my life. We drove the next day to Big Bend, arriving around noon. We ate; then it got interesting.

Humping it up a mountain with a pack almost did me in. I had to learn to accept and then ask for help from the young ones. That meant everyone else in the group. At the age of 74, I was older than any of their fathers. One of the leaders wore a prosthetic leg – a souvenir of combat. Another participant had damage to both eyes and was legally blind. All the participants, including me, had a current diagnosis of post-traumatic stress syndrome.

I soon realized I was never going to complete the expedition without help. Accepting I needed help was humbling, but the staff was very diplomatic in easing me through that barrier. So, I began to ask when I needed it and looked for opportunities to help others with the lessons age brings. And maybe even help somebody up when they fell.

Three days up, around, and down, the Chisos Mountain's beautiful wilderness fatigued every muscle in my body. Exhausted, I slept well on Tuesday night, October 8th, in the Rio Grande Village Campground. The next morning, I woke energized, ready for the next half of the expedition. I thought a bit of yoga would perhaps soothe my weary muscles and allow me to meditate about the experiences I had endured. And possibly contemplate the next four days, starting after breakfast, when we would travel thirty-three miles, on the river in the canyons between Texas and Mexico, in kayaks.

At 6:30 AM, on Wednesday, October 9th, 2019, after freshening up, I remember starting my usual yoga practice. At some point, I lost immediate awareness of my position or how long I had held it. The last move I recall doing was the tree pose with my hands at heart center. Then I felt the first salty tear.

The tear slid down my right cheek and brought me back into semi-awareness. The most intense joyfulness filled every part of my being. An explosion of feeling like nothing I had ever experienced. Joy, pure joy. Beyond the intensity of holding my daughter for the first time. Way past the thrill of marrying Jasmine, the love of my life. An overwhelming merging of pure sensations and a mortal body accustomed to only slight variations of feelings–unless provoked. A perfect union of being present in the moment and an event with no beginning or end. It was the most real experience of my life and the most exciting. I was at one with the universe.

My eyes were open, but I could not see. I was outdoors and knew I was near a flock of birds noisily awakening from their night of rest, but I could no longer hear. I knew there were people cooking breakfast, but I could no longer smell. I could feel my emotions, but I could not feel my body touching the ground.

No one could feel this great, I later thought. A happiness that brought tears to my eyes with no apparent trigger. Pure bliss. No separation of my physical body and the wild emotions uplifting my entire being. I remember smiling as the tears welled up in my eyes and fell on my shirt.

I have no idea how long the event lasted or how I got from the campground's fringes back to our group's site. "I think something just happened," as I looked at two of our leaders seated at a picnic table. They glanced up from their coffee cups and waited for me to say something more. "I can't explain what happened to me, but I'm going to give it a shot and say I feel like I've been reborn." I knew that wasn't the right phrase, but it was a start. I had generally given up on organized religion in my teen years and shuddered to think I had experienced some sort of religious reawakening. I walked away from the table and went into my tent and lay down. At least I think I did.

I wasn't quite sure what to do about this "rebirthing" experience I had but knew the group was a safe place to express feelings and tell others what had happened. We shared our thoughts about the initial portion of the expedition at a campfire that first night on the Rio Grande. We repeated this sharing over the next few nights. We bonded as a group, and I focused on being grateful for the help, how challenged I was by the physical demands on my body, and for what had happened to me Wednesday morning in the campground. Most of the vets gave me their thoughts about what happened. They made various suggestions either in a group setting around the campfire, or one-on-one with me. Some suggested it was Jesus talking to me. Perhaps I was being repaid with good karma for my hundreds of hours of volunteer work. I even thought maybe my 97-year-old mother had let go and passed.

No way to find out about the latter–we had no communications with the outside world. Plenty of time to reflect. In the end, I settled on a word I thought best described what happened to me–rapture. As I said the word rapture, I saw expressions of wonder on the other participants' faces.

Merriam-Webster defines rapture in the following ways:

1: an expression or manifestation of ecstasy or passion

2a: a state or experience of being carried away by overwhelming emotion

b: a mystical experience in which the spirit is exalted to a knowledge of divine things

3: often capitalized: the final assumption of Christians into heaven during the end-time according to Christian theology

Rapture–yes, that was the right word, even though I was not religious. I cannot recall ever using the phrase rapture verbally or in writing throughout my entire life. Having now consulted various sources on the meaning of the word, I accept the first two definitions and think it includes precisely what happened to me. But why me? Why now? And what was I supposed to do with it? I vowed to understand the experience and pledged to continue my investigation when I got back to civilization.

Who to tell and what to say to them ran through my mind as I rode in the van back to Midland. When we got into cell phone range, I texted Jasmine and told her I was still alive and would be headed home to Corrales the following day. I said nothing about the rapture, unsure how she would react.

The seven-hour drive home allowed me time to formulate what I wanted to tell Jasmine. I first recounted what happened during the nine-day expedition. I tiptoed into what happened on Wednesday morning, October 9th. Jasmine listened carefully and said that she knew something like that would happen. She added that she knew I had to take part in this expedition–she had never seen me so motivated to get myself into a semblance of good physical shape before I left for Big Bend.

I would not be satisfied until I had exhausted looking into all possible explanations of my experience. Why me? Why now? And what was I supposed to do with it? I sought out very close friends and family. I contacted a spiritual leader who is extremely hard to reach but suddenly was available for a two-hour conversation by phone. I consulted my psychologist (who knows me inside out), nurses, doctors, a psychic, a minister, and my yoga teachers. I went to my usual Thursday morning writing group at the Albuquerque VA hospital and met a young veteran who had never been there before. The young man started a discussion in which he recounted an experience he called an explosion of good feelings–being re-baptized. It could have been my story. He came to one more group session, and I have never seen him again. People who I needed became available and were interested in my experience.

All these people told me that what happened was not unique. It was unusual, but not unknown. Mystical events like this have happened to people all over the world for eons. One expert told me of the correlation between the body's and the mind's fatiguing and opening the body and mind to new experiences. Another said God is joy, and if I had experienced such an overwhelming feeling of pleasure... well, I was left to connect the dots myself. I started to think about all the Christian hymns and teachings that emphasize joy.

I did not post what happened on October 9th on my social media platforms. Only after some time passed, I started to open up to people I thought would accept my recounting of this story as truth without wondering if I had just flown in from a parallel universe. Those with whom I have shared my rapture experience have urged me to write about it.

Let's address the questions I posed:

Why me? The short answer is because I answered an ad and decided with my right (intuitive) brain and pure gut instinct to participate in an intense, physically demanding expedition in the wilderness. Had I done a careful, time-consuming analysis of what I was going to face and understand the challenges ahead, I might have decided not to participate. But I acted instinctively and irrationally. An impulse guided me to join this trek without fully understanding the consequences. In retrospect, I'm glad I did, and I know I'm a better person for having done so. I have always trusted my instincts, and this time, some part of me understood why I needed to participate. My mind learned later.

Why now? Because I placed myself in a situation where I was in a new and pleasing physical environment, where I fatigued my body and made the switch to accept and even ask for help. I was open for something to happen to me on the morning of October 9th, 2019. I had worked for months to get ready for the expedition. For three days, I had been physically and emotionally challenged. My defensive walls were down, and I had been asking for and accepting help. I was surrounded by beautiful nature for an extended time. Equally important, I had no internet access. Instead, I was executing familiar yoga positions and meditating. Had each of these conditions not existed, the rapture might never have happened. It was like a perfect storm–just not at all threatening. Perhaps a higher power had heard me ask for help and answered in a way I could not possibly imagine.

What am I supposed to do with it? Why was this happening to me at the age of 74? Then I replayed the mental recording of my fellow veterans who completed the experience. Each of them felt their own unique joy. I watched disabled veterans having fun cannon-balling with each other in the river. I empathized with returning soldiers acting like they were healthy. Perhaps my most memorable experience was following our legally blind Marine paddling his kayak down the river, in the lead, singing with his head bobbing from side to side like Ray Charles. Each veteran was touched by joy differently. That, too, gave me pleasure. I choke up every time I relive seeing these broken men and women happy. They gave all they could for our country and will forever pay the price for their service. They deserved joy and positive reinforcement.

We all have gifts. Mine include successfully flying off aircraft carriers, day or night, in the middle of the ocean with nowhere else to go. I was good at it and enjoyed being at the top of my game. My aviation career shaped my post-flying life. I rarely back down from a challenge, and I am glad for this expedition. I went with my gut. Navy pilots have an expression: kick the tires, light the fire, brief on guard. That's what I did–figured it out as I was doing it.

Another gift is my ability to put emotions and experiences on paper and create an effect in the mind's eye of a reader. Bottling up this experience is simply the wrong thing to do. There are messages from this experience for the reader. And I am supposed to share this experience with you. That is what I learned. Offering the event to readers or listeners with no expectation of anything other than to show joy was possible to me, a disabled vet, at the ripe old age of 74.

No matter how bleak the circumstances, joy is possible in your life. Open to receive it, and don't be afraid of taking a chance. Let down your defensive walls – but be in a safe environment when you do so.

Not everything found on Facebook is right for you – but responding to this ad changed my life. Your joy may not occur in Texas, at a campground, or while doing yoga, but it may come to you in ways you would not anticipate. Staying at home, hunkered down, expecting the worst is not a likely path to experience joy or to receive unexpected healing.

I did not expect to find rapture when I went on this expedition. I don't think you can seek and discover rapture. It just happens. Rapture found me. My experience was a unity between myself and a higher power. Perhaps nearing the supreme consciousness, or a peek at the Omega Point, envisaged by the Jesuit priest Pierre Teilhard de Chardin. My rapture was brief, but it was real. My rapture was, without a doubt, the most unusual experience I have ever had.

I passed the test. I performed well past what my logical brain would have said I was capable of doing. Who arranged for this test? I answered the ad, but I did not understand the degree to which I would be tested. Was it pure chance? Or was it part of a divine pattern designed to reveal itself in a way that would mean more than any sermon or words on a page?

I am forever grateful for having been challenged. For without that challenge, I might never have experienced what I did. Without that experience, I would not be telling this story. And, with that story, perhaps you might think about truths that cannot be explained with the logical mind.

About Jim Tritten

Jim Tritten is a retired Navy pilot who lives in a small village in New Mexico with his Danish artist/author wife and four cats.

Also by Jim Tritten

Jim has published six books and over three hundred chapters, short stories, essays, articles, and government technical reports.

Connect with Jim Tritten

http://www.amazon.com/James-John-Tritten/e/B001KHVMCM

https://www.facebook.com/jimtrittenauthor/

http://www.goodreads.com/author/show/
2487183.James_J_Tritten

4

LOST&FOUND

NIKA JORDAN ROSE

PROLOGUE

An empty space.

Pitch black.

Nothingness.

A faint outline of LOST sitting on the ground.

Stillness.

Silence.

It seems to go on forever.

LOST doesn't seem afraid.

She surrenders willingly to the dark.

A moment.

She gently strokes her arms.

With each touch parts of her body seem to disappear.

Stroke.

Stroke.

Stroke.

The faint outline fades.

Total blackness.

An eternal void.

END OF SCENE

EPISODE 1

Lights up.

A grocery store.

Ambient noise of the other customers but we cannot see them.

LOST enters.

Coddling a small red basket.

The ambient noise becomes deafening.

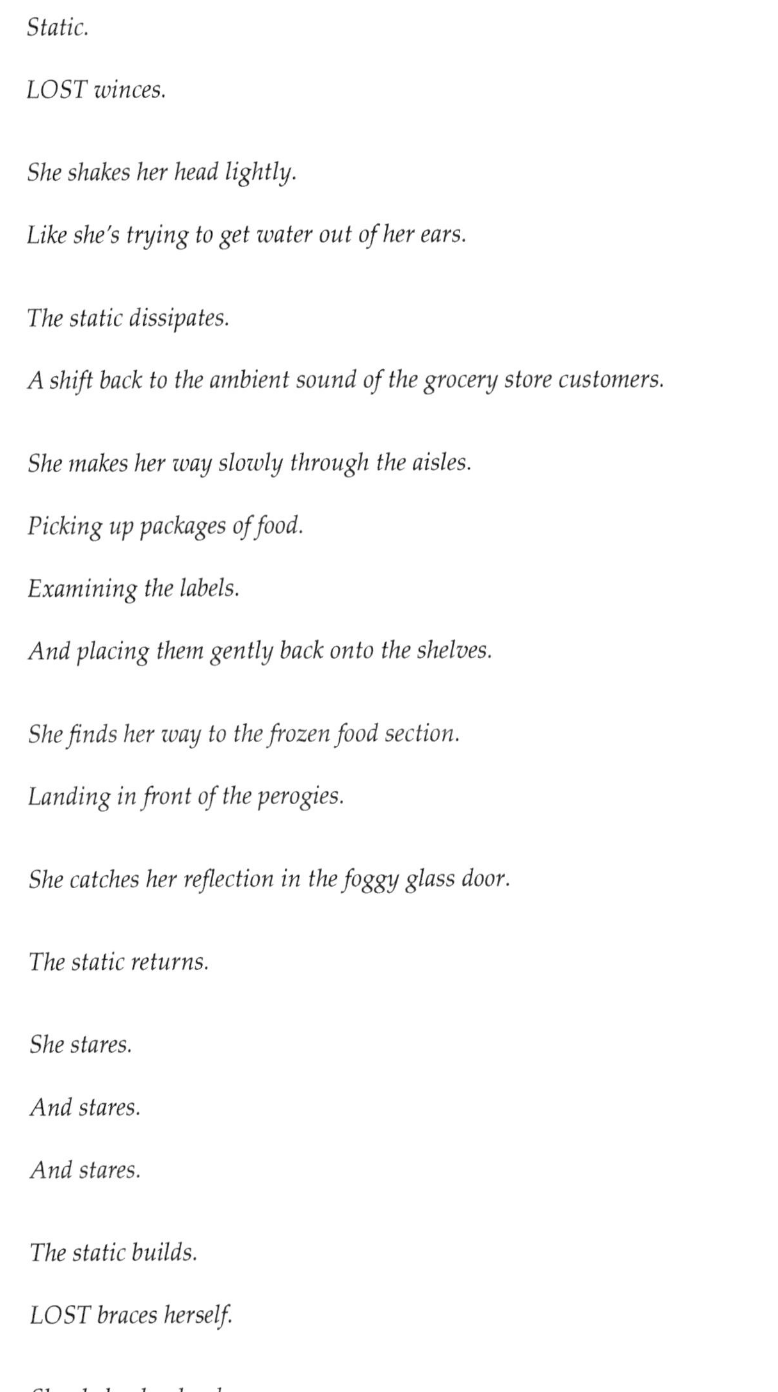

Static.

LOST winces.

She shakes her head lightly.

Like she's trying to get water out of her ears.

The static dissipates.

A shift back to the ambient sound of the grocery store customers.

She makes her way slowly through the aisles.

Picking up packages of food.

Examining the labels.

And placing them gently back onto the shelves.

She finds her way to the frozen food section.

Landing in front of the perogies.

She catches her reflection in the foggy glass door.

The static returns.

She stares.

And stares.

And stares.

The static builds.

LOST braces herself.

She shakes her head.

And blinks.

But the static does not dissipate.

A moment.

She robotically walks past the cashier with her empty basket.

And exits.

END OF SCENE

EPISODE 2

Lights up.

A tiny apartment.

Clearly meant for one.

Barren.

Devoid of life.

With the exception of a thin purple yoga mat laid out on the hardwood floor.

LOST enters from the bathroom.

She's wearing a large tshirt and unimpressive underwear.

She sits on the mat.

She breathes.

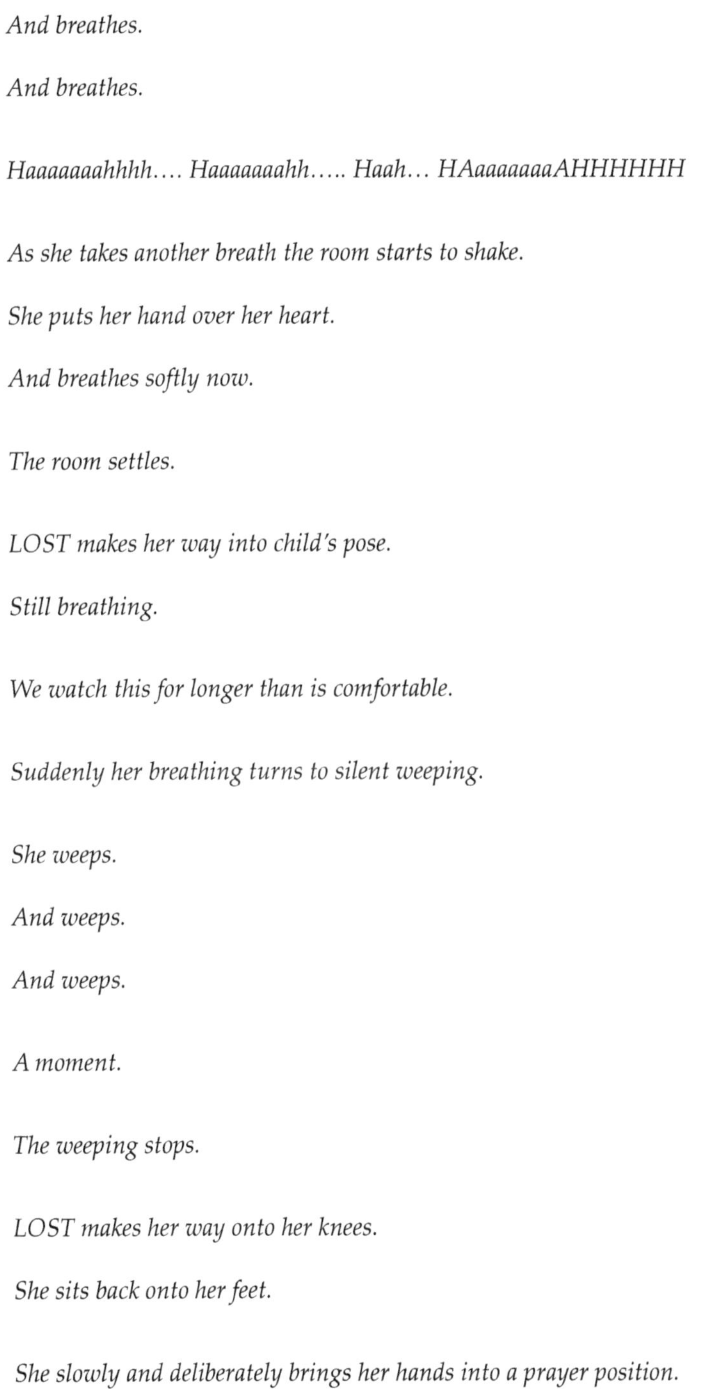

And breathes.

And breathes.

Haaaaaaahhhh…. Haaaaaaahh….. Haah… HAaaaaaaaAHHHHHH

As she takes another breath the room starts to shake.

She puts her hand over her heart.

And breathes softly now.

The room settles.

LOST makes her way into child's pose.

Still breathing.

We watch this for longer than is comfortable.

Suddenly her breathing turns to silent weeping.

She weeps.

And weeps.

And weeps.

A moment.

The weeping stops.

LOST makes her way onto her knees.

She sits back onto her feet.

She slowly and deliberately brings her hands into a prayer position.

She brings her gaze down.

And clenches her eyes shut.

The way she has seen people do in movies and at Christmas Eve service.

She waits.

Silence.

She breaks her hands from the position.

And looks up toward the sky.

She weeps.

And weeps.

And weeps.

A beat.

A change.

LOST begins to shake lightly.

And as if she feels arms holding her from behind she puts her hands on her own shoulders.

Her weeping is different now.

She smiles.

She looks up toward the sky.

And silently mouths thank you.

END OF SCENE

EPISODE 3

Lights up.

An unfamiliar room.

There are stacks of psychology books piled all over the space.

LOST sits in an armchair.

Across from her is another identical, yet empty, armchair.

LOST
Sometimes I wonder how long it would take
For someone to notice
Like if I had a heart attack
Or slipped in the shower
Or was murdered by an armed robber
Would I just rot?
Rot
Rotttttt
I'm 858 miles from home
In an empty apartment
In my 'void'
(that's what I like to call it)
How many unanswered calls would it take before someone got on a plane?
Would the neighbors hear?
Or question why they hadn't seen anyone walking up the stairs in awhile?
And if they did hear or question would they care enough to call someone?

What I'm trying to say is that/
I have no one in this city that would notice whether I'm dead or alive
So
I guess that's why I called you
Because maybe if I don't show up for a session
Or send you a check
You would call
Or stop by
For a wellness check
Or something that would keep my corpse from decomposing on the hardwood floor next to a yoga mat.
Sorry-
That's probably a really weird way to introduce myself.

She stares at the empty chair.

She smiles faintly.

END OF SCENE

EPISODE 4

Lights up.

A classroom.

Two desks sit in the front facing the student desks.

We hear the ambient sound of the students but do not see them.

LOST enters.

She sits in one of the desks up front.

The ambient noise of the students intensifies.

Static.

LOST winces.

It grows.

She hangs onto the desk for dear life.

A painful moment of stillness.

FOUND enters hurriedly.

He is reading something as he walks.

He sits down in the other desk up front.

He pulls a pencil from behind his ear and vigorously underlines something.

He breathes.

And closes the book.

He looks over at LOST.

He clocks her wincy face.

He stares at her.

And stares.

And stares.

And stares.

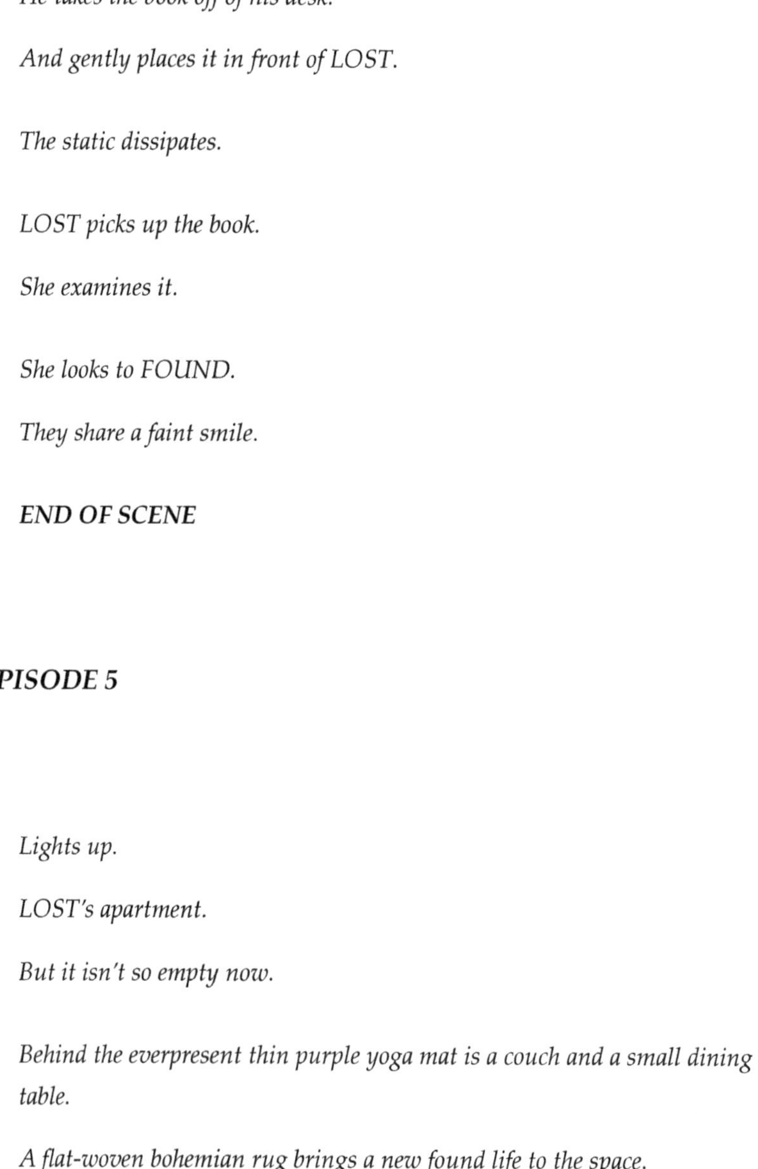

He takes the book off of his desk.

And gently places it in front of LOST.

The static dissipates.

LOST picks up the book.

She examines it.

She looks to FOUND.

They share a faint smile.

END OF SCENE

EPISODE 5

Lights up.

LOST's apartment.

But it isn't so empty now.

Behind the everpresent thin purple yoga mat is a couch and a small dining table.

A flat-woven bohemian rug brings a new found life to the space.

LOST enters from the bathroom.

There is an energy in her we have not yet observed until this point.

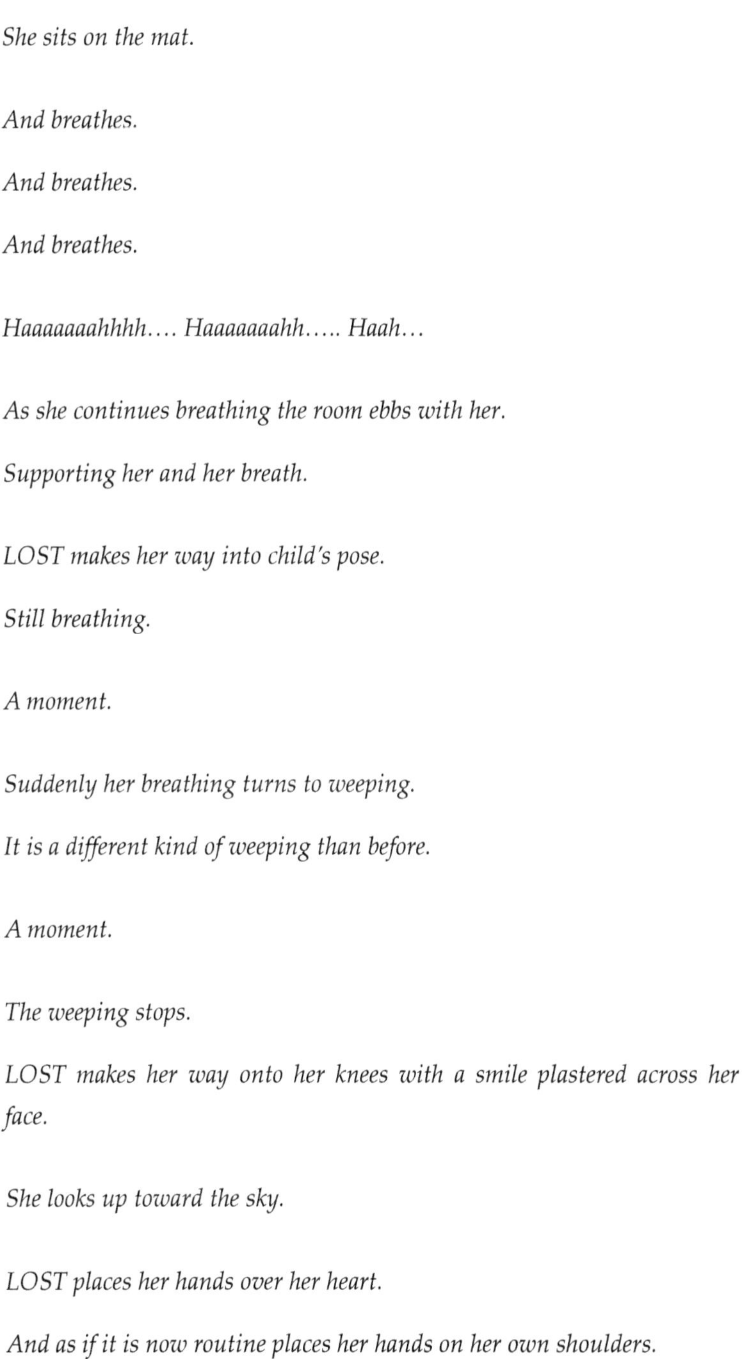

She sits on the mat.

And breathes.

And breathes.

And breathes.

Haaaaaaahhhh…. Haaaaaaahh….. Haah…

As she continues breathing the room ebbs with her.

Supporting her and her breath.

LOST makes her way into child's pose.

Still breathing.

A moment.

Suddenly her breathing turns to weeping.

It is a different kind of weeping than before.

A moment.

The weeping stops.

LOST makes her way onto her knees with a smile plastered across her face.

She looks up toward the sky.

LOST places her hands over her heart.

And as if it is now routine places her hands on her own shoulders.

She looks back up toward the sky.

And silently mouths thank you.

END OF SCENE

EPISODE 6

Lights up.

A therapist's apartment.

LOST sits in an armchair.

Across from her is another identical armchair.

This time it houses an eldery woman with a kind demeanor.

LOST
Do you remember last year when I got locked out of my apartment?
And my next session I came in weeping
Because all I could think about was that if I couldn't get back in-
I'd have nowhere to go
I'd have no one to stay with- you know
So ever since that day I've become obsessive about checking my apartment door before I leave
(because I accidentally deadbolted it from the inside and that's how I got locked out- I guess that part doesn't really matter but yeah)
I would check it at least 3 times before I left for the day

I would walk out of my door and close it behind me.
And then unlock it.
And then close it.
And unlock.
Close and unlock.
Just to triple check.
And I even started keeping another set of keys in my backpack.
In case I lost my purse.
THAT'S how fucking terrified I was that I would get locked out again
And have no one to call
No one to stay with
(well I guess you but that's just depressing)
I'm telling you this to say that I left my apartment this morning
AND I didn't check the door!
Not even once
I didn't even check to see if I had my keys!
Because today if I walk up my six flights of stairs and my door is accidentally bolted from the inside
I'll just walk the 8 blocks down
And ring the buzzer
And he'll be waiting for me
And I feel-
So relieved.

END OF SCENE

EPILOGUE

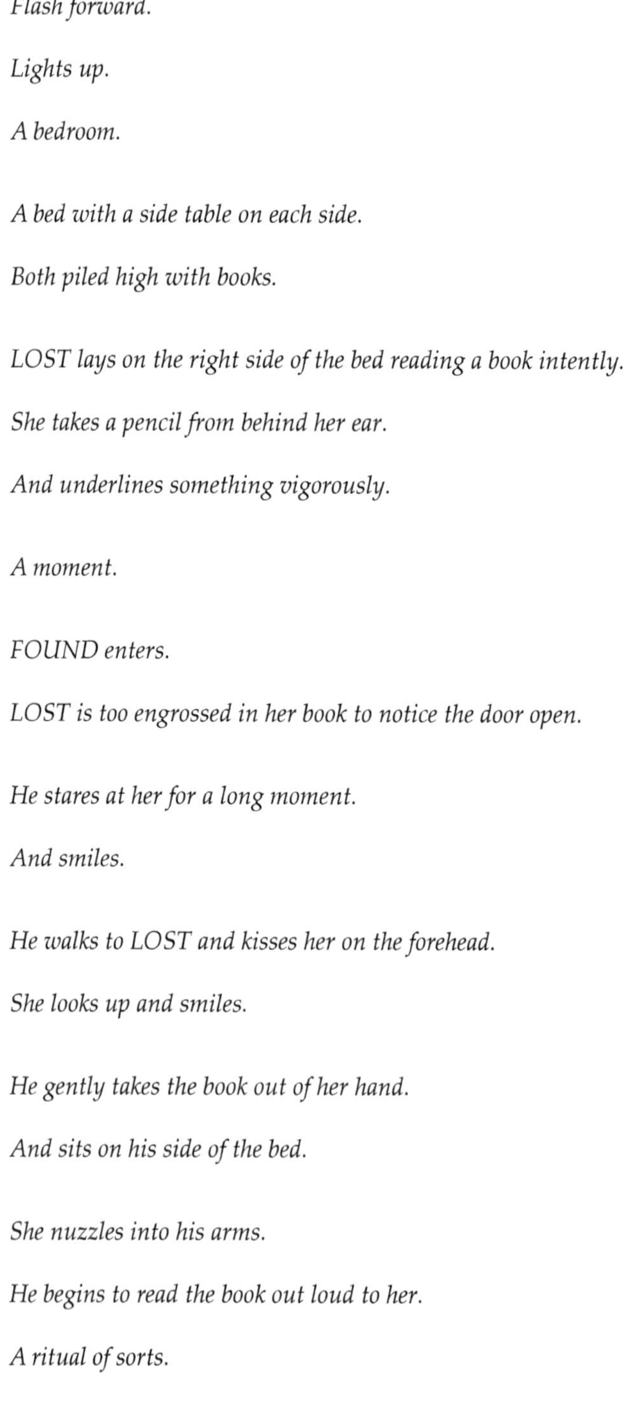

Flash forward.

Lights up.

A bedroom.

A bed with a side table on each side.

Both piled high with books.

LOST lays on the right side of the bed reading a book intently.

She takes a pencil from behind her ear.

And underlines something vigorously.

A moment.

FOUND enters.

LOST is too engrossed in her book to notice the door open.

He stares at her for a long moment.

And smiles.

He walks to LOST and kisses her on the forehead.

She looks up and smiles.

He gently takes the book out of her hand.

And sits on his side of the bed.

She nuzzles into his arms.

He begins to read the book out loud to her.

A ritual of sorts.

We listen to this for a long moment.

The lights slowly fade to black.

END OF PLAY

About Nika Jordan Rose

Nika Rose is an NYC-based dramaturg and aspiring literary manager. During her time at Marymount Manhattan College, she held multiple literary positions, including her current role as Literary Assistant for Bret Adams Ltd, a boutique theatrical agency. In addition to her experience as a literary administrator, she is also a writer in her own right. Her short plays *Dissociation Station*, *Sinking*, and *LOST&FOUND* are explorations of the visceral, physical touch, and the deeply human need for connection in a self-isolated world.

Connect with Nika Jordan Rose

Instagram: @nikajordanxo

5

The Best Time of My Life

SWAN ROSE

When I try to think of the greatest time or event of my life, my mind floods with images. I fixate on each one for different amounts of time. While some are fleeting and draw a quick smile, others demand a longer thoughtful gaze into what once was. When one has lived a life such as mine, how do you even begin to choose one shining moment? Not only is it a daunting task, but it somehow feels as if it would diminish others. As I ponder this, the stream of seemingly never-ending memories makes it abundantly clear.

They say right before you die, your whole life flashes before your eyes. If that is true, I sincerely hope the perception of that moment feels as if it goes on forever. Suppose I can revel in the best moments of my life all at once. Surely this would be the best time in my life, from all my most cherished moments with my loved ones to moments that were mine and mine alone. I wonder, would they play in order or bounce around in time frantically?

My current state of mind might have the answer to this as I sit here, unable to stop the flood. It races to all memories in no particular order of time or importance, the only constant being they are all cherished. I become increasingly aware of one gift I have been blessed with, that being the ability to take such long-lasting pleasure from seemingly small moments. While just something to smile about, if that lasts a lifetime, that is not small in any way.

This is not to say I don't have many big moments as I indeed do. The birth of both of my children looms large, as does any time I have ever spent with either. I sang to Shy, my first child, as I rocked her in the hospital room, the song "Gettin Better." The lyrics hitting home as my life at the time was rudderless and lacked real meaning. Singing this would become a bedtime ritual that she demanded for many years. I was never sure who liked it more, her or me. I am pretty sure it was me.

As she grew older and we lived apart, her visits for Holidays and the summer were like an oasis in the desert. No matter how old she becomes, I will always see that little girl wearing the princess outfit she loved so much. And I remember how we would watch the same movie all summer long. She never grew tired of them, and I never grew tired of spending that time with her. We would often recite them line by line with each other. The excitement on that little face when I knew them too was priceless. My favorite memories, however, will always be what we called pretty woman day. One day every summer we would shop till we dropped. She would come out of countless dressing rooms and spin and look into the mirrors. I would sit and watch and wait. I would wait for that moment when she would stop and look over to me and say, "daddy, I love it."

The smile and excitement on her face was something I could not get enough of. If you are thinking that I spoiled her on these days. Boy, would you be correct.

• • •

When people ask me about my children and who they are as people, I always say Shy is my Bob Marley child. The memory I share to illustrate this is always the same. I called her when she was still a teenager just to check-in. We talked for quite a while and I noticed a lot of wind blowing into her cell phone. I asked where she was and why it was so windy. She said, "oh, I am walking beside the road going home." "Why are you walking?" I asked. She proceeds to say, very casually, that her car just blew up. You know, when the smoke rolls out from the hood. I say "I am so sorry, babe!" to which she replies "No worries." Everything in her tone said she meant it. This story never fails to elicit a laugh.

Now that she is much older, watching her be a mom is so enjoyable. Many of the old charismatics of the young Shy are still well intact. Even with all the stress of mothering two children, she remains the sweet happy girl she always has been. But now I get to watch all the unexpected new qualities as well. Getting to spend time watching her balance, it all never fails to impress. So far from the girl who rode in the U-Haul with me across the country. For anyone that knows Shy, it would come as no surprise that we talked the entire way. We still talk about how we played spot the hottie game. And how she won when she yelled five hotties at a Jeep full of guys. A game she started, of course. I am smiling even as I write this.

While I lament at all the time we missed together, I feel so grateful. Who else gets to watch their 10-year-old child protect the car by acting like she knew karate when cars drove by, all while exclaiming, "That's right, keep driving, sucker!" She was so little and so intense the drivers could be seen smiling and laughing as they went by. Or having her at four use a payphone to call 911 because her pretend cat was missing. Umm baby, hangup, let's get out of here! There are so many memories of car rides and talks with her, young and old. How could I possibly ask for more?

• • •

My youngest, Nika Jordan Rose, I can't even type her name without using the full name. I know it seems silly, but it has taken on a life of its own. One of my favorite small memories of her was when she was two. We were in a store, and I had her in a cart. As I rolled by a rack of dresses, she pointed to one and said, "Daddy, that's cool." A woman nearby heard her and looked to see who said it. She was smiling as she turned to look. When she saw how young Nika was, she looked at me with her eyes wide as if to say *wow*. Then she chuckled and walked off. These kinds of moments continued for years. In fact, from ages 3 to 5, co-workers would ask several times a week for Nika stories. "What did she say now?" they would ask. I would tell them of words she used seemingly out of nowhere and in the right context. Or how, at four, she was addicted to HGTV. I would wake up from working the late shift and walk out to see this young girl transfixed to the TV. I would look at the screen and it would be people remodeling a bathroom. It always felt so surreal. One day I came out, and she was drawing, and I thought, oh, this is more normal. Then she told me she was drawing up new designs for redoing our kitchen. She was making sure to increase our counter space, of course!

When I describe her to those that ask, I say she is my serious child.

She has always wanted to succeed and be better than she probably should be at whatever age she was at the time, only comparing herself to someone she viewed as better. Whether that was correct or not didn't matter. In her mind, they were. Even if they were much older there was not an excuse. I tried on many occasions to ease this concern of not being good enough. But, to no avail (and sometimes to my detriment!), she needed to be better. She used this to fuel her and propel her forward. She had shown very early signs of creativity. At first, it was in her writing for school. Her focus went to theater quickly as she started being in school plays at an early age. I will never forget watching her play Becky, a perky cheerleader in elementary school. I watched her bounce around with her pom-poms and talk like an 80's valley girl. She was so spot-on that I and everyone there had to laugh. It was one scene, but one of the most memorable. Parents or faculty would ask me which one of the kids was mine and, when I told them, their faces would light up. "She's so funny," they would say, "Is she really a cheerleader?" To which I would have to chuckle and say, "No, she is not." It was so unlike her personality that I was left thinking she can actually do this.

I loved watching her do anything. Gymnastics when she was tiny. Volleyball was a lot of fun in middle school. But nothing compared to watching her progress as an actor and as a singer. Seeing the fruits of all of her labor was rewarding as a parent. I even eventually found myself watching her play a role that was based during World War II, with her hairstyle and her character having a southern accent. As soon as she came out the first night, all I could think of was my Mema. Mema being of that generation, southern, and with Nika having such a strong resemblance to her, it was undeniable. She was so dominant and forceful and, yet, still funny. One monologue was so over the top it was like a roller coaster feeling the audience reaction every night. First, a stunned whoa sitting back and then adjusting and leaning forward, enjoying it until they were at last hit with a punchline that landed every show. And of course, this would be the one time I could not get a video. But this role remains burned into my brain, and it still brings me joy. I know in my heart Mema was very proud.

Her high school role in "In the Heights" will always be in my mind as a kind of coming-out party with so many people, including my wife's family, starting to see how skilled she already was. I say skilled and not talented because talent can sometimes come easy. Her role as Abuela allowed her to perform a song basically alone on the stage with others walking around in the background. She displayed such confidence and command of the stage that I was again surprised by the level she had reached once again. As she hit the crescendo, she had us all in the palm of her hand. Every single night she won over the crowd, and you could hear the people after the applause died down talking. "Wow, that was amazing," I could hear. The feeling of her getting the attention she deserved is as large a part of reliving this experience as any.

She has worked hard to better herself her entire life. So hard at times, it has worried me. I took her to lunch once to discuss this. I told her I was proud that she pushed herself, but I didn't want her to be so fixated on how much she wanted to improve that she missed out on enjoying what she was doing at the time she was doing it. She looked me in the eyes and said that "every one that is great is like this," and "if I want to be great, I have to be this way." One, how do you combat that? And two, how can you not respect it? These are moments outside of the roles and the shows that she later directed that stand independently and perhaps larger in some ways. Like when we were touring Indiana University and had a moment alone. I said, "I know this is not where you want to go, but they seem to have a pretty good program." She shrugged and said, "Yeah, they are ok." I said, "Well, maybe if it is good but not great, it'll be easier to get parts." She looked disgusted and said, "I would rather be the worst person in the best program than the star of a horrible program." Again, how can you not love that?

Watching her continue to grow not only as a person, but as an artist is an amazing thing. She has a crazy blend of creativity and logical decision making ability that is rare to see. I am enjoying the ride and watching her life as if it's a movie. At this point, I have no idea where this will all go. I don't think she does either. But does it really matter? Is that really the point?

My mind now switches gears as I am all of sudden young again. I am sitting in the break room in college. I am sitting with friends and someone is talking. I am not paying attention as I watch a girl walk by that I had never seen before. I watch until she is gone. A friend looks back at me and says, "Did you see that?" Yes. Yes, I did. Now, to make this clearer for you, many can look cute just walking by. But a very, very few can also manage to look so sweet at the same time. After that, whenever she was around, my friend would say, "there she is." And I would always say, "Oh, I see her," because you can trust me when I say I already had. Eventually I would meet Alicia at a party, and she was just as sweet as she had looked the first time I saw her. I was early to a party at her apartment. Of course, being as nice as she was, she let me in anyway. I was the only one there as her and her roommate were busy getting ready.

I remember so vividly watching her as she kept coming out to the living room to look at her new outfit in the full-length mirror. Getting irritated, she said that it never looks as good as it does in the store. Well, I wasn't at the store, but she looked great. At the time I had no idea that we would end up dating through a long, long, long list of unexpected turns of events. Then, when we started dating, we knew we would break up because she was moving away. But I was blessed and she decided to come back so we could live together. And that eventually led to us getting married and having Nika.

Ours is such a long story as to how all of this unfolded, but to say we are the love that was not supposed to be is an understatement. And now, all of these years later, we are left with so many beautiful memories. Some are just between us, like all the drives in Georgia with no idea where we were going. Armed with no maps and no GPS, we would set out to drive to parts unknown. Out in the middle of nowhere with me driving and Alicia saying, "Ummm, take a left... or right," at any remote crossroads we came across. I love those memories, but I am still surprised we always managed to find our way home. Thank god she has a good sense of direction!

Our first date was one for the record books! I had not asked her out and showed up at her apartment on Halloween night. Several of our friends were there and no one was planning on going anywhere. I asked her to go out with me. She said she had to get up early. "You want to hang out here with us?" she asked. I knew if I could just get the others to go, she would too. Knowing our friends as I did, I knew just the thing. I said, "Hey guys, let's go. I will pay for everyone's drinks!" Never have you seen a group of twenty-somethings move so fast.

I looked at Alicia and smiled, and she said "Okay, okay, I will." The rest, as they say, is history. Well, except to say that many memories that will play to show my life will be of this night. Besides how happy I was to be with her, Miami Beach on Halloween night is something to behold. I explain it to people as a sort of Mardi Gras. I determined that many of the most, shall we say, "unique" individuals save money all year to spend on their costumes. How could I not recall the man dressed as a giant insect running up against all of the windows of a hotel lobby as if he could not get out. Or what I called The Legion of Doom! This was a group of guys donning monk robes. Their Leader had hands that were glowing and a long cape that was being carried at the end by an extremely muscular woman. She was wearing what most resembled an amazon outfit. They were walking slowly, which made it that much more intimidating.

But the moment of the night was the three drag queens driving a pink jeep with the top off. One was standing up with a microphone that was sparkling from fake diamonds. Lip-syncing to Cher's "If I Could Turn Back Time" while the wind made it all seem so much like an actual video shoot. After dropping the mic on the street, our friend Christie ran out in heels and gave it back. The running appeared to be no small feat, but the show must go on.

Our trip to St. Lucia will always be there in the great time's list! It goes along with so many nights out with our friends, including getting her to come to some concerts she would otherwise never go to. As I grow older, I have changed in so many ways. But in some ways I am still the same kid she met. It makes me so happy that I can say the same about her. There are a lot of reasons why we are the person for each other. But, honestly, this could be the most important one of all. Living life is easy, but really living your life is the true pursuit. One has to have the right partner, or a high level of happiness can never be reached.

While these moments seem like so much already–an embarrassment of riches–I have still many great moments outside of those with my family. One I have always referred to as one of the greatest nights of my life happened in college. It was the kind of night that seemed to go on forever and had so many twists and turns that it felt like a movie. It started fairly innocently with a friend asking me if I wanted to go for a ride and get off Miami Beach. At that point, I didn't have a car and walked everywhere. The thought of going somewhere else sounded good. We drove for a while and I asked where we were going and he said, “I want to show you something.” After a while, he pulled into a convenience store, driving around the back. I asked, “What are we doing here?” He said, “I will be right back.” He came back with bags of chips and dropped his truck's tailgate and said, “Sit here.” After we got up in the truck, he started throwing the chips out in the grass in front of us. After a minute, Some of the biggest raccoons I have ever seen came out. He said, “I found them by accident the other night and wanted to show someone.” They were so calm that I walked out among them in the grass and, after a while, sat down. To this day I can't believe I did that and would never recommend it! But I am glad I did, because the only thing I have from this night is a picture of a Metal/Hippie-looking kid with long hair and ripped jeans sitting on the ground with Raccoons all around him. This, however, was just the beginning of the night.

After we left, we drove around Miami for a while. At some point, I realized that every sign I saw was in Spanish. I had never seen or experienced that before. Seeing large billboards in another language made me suddenly feel as if I was in another country. I had always enjoyed being submerged into different cultures, but this took it to another level. Driving around in the city at night made me feel free. I could have done that all night. But eventually we went back to his apartment building, which was full of other students. As usual, several parties were going on. Music could be heard down the hallways and floors coming out of many apartments. Kids were in the hallways and walking in and out of apartments as if they were bar-hopping. This all was a typical night for us. I walked in and out of doorways, reliving the same experience each time, always looking to see who was in the extreme darkness of the candlelit rooms.

I was drinking whatever was offered, slapping or hugging people, talking about what music played with approval or condemnation. Going to a music school makes for harsh critics on the taste of others.

After a couple of hours, I bumped into one of my favorite people Frank. Frank usually did not come to these and lived in Miami normally, so he did not live with students. This also meant he drove everywhere. He predictably wanted to leave and asked if I wanted to drive around. Of course I did, but now I was in the mood to keep the party going. Because of this, I talked two friends that were typically wallflowers into coming with us.

We drove all over, even ending up in the Fort Lauderdale airport somehow.

I rode shotgun as we had a rolling party with the music blasting. I have to say that, after a long time, while we were having a great time in the front seat, my wallflower friends in the back seat were not. They wanted to go home, but I wanted the night to last forever.

The lasting moment of the night and perhaps my life was when we went through the Fort Lauderdale tunnel. On the first pass through, I leaned out the window to scream with a whiskey bottle in my hand. I leaned too far and Mary grabbed my shirt and pulled me back in. She said, "Dude, stand up through the sunroof." I did, and it was incredible. The wind was blowing through my hair and the echo from my yelling. I made him drive through it at least four more times. That night, like all others, eventually had to end. In this case, the sun was coming up.

There, of course, are so many more long lasting imprints of important or just fun moments. Like singing for the first time on stage and in front of that same brutal music school crowd. Still hard to believe, I choose to do that.

Writing poetry, making my website, and reading some of the people's reactions in countries I will never go to. Even having an artist from Brazil make a painting because of one of them. I look forward to all my future moments. But at the same time, I know that if I had to leave this world tomorrow. I would not feel cheated. I have, and I am, living the best time of my life.

About Swan Rose

Swan is a former musician who is now focused on writing poetry and short stories. He has been writing in some form since he was

17. He enjoys writing about the human condition. While much of this can at worst be very sad and at best be serious, this is not all that encompasses him. And it does not represent his constant state of mind. Many of his pieces are directly influenced by his life or moments in time from it. Some are indirectly influenced and some at not at all. He says which ones are and which ones are not is really not important. The point he has come to realize is to create a picture or feeling with words, one that is both fairly easy to digest and easily relatable. If not relatable by your own experience perhaps through the experience of a significant other.

Also by Swan Rose

Inspiration Speaks Volume 1

Connect with Swan Rose

blackswanpoetry.wordpress.com/

About the Editor

JK Larkin is a Long Island based writer and recent graduate of Marymount Manhattan College. On top of his position as Literary Manager and Editor of *The Red Penguin Collection,* JK works at The Mary Louis Academy as the coach of their Speech & Debate Team, coaching students to perform excerpts of dramatic literature, prose, and poetry for weekly competitions on both the local and national levels. His body of work draws heavily upon themes of queerness, existentialism, morality, and the struggle to connect in a deeply divided world. This past year, JK published his first two collections, ***not kidding.*** and ***Side Street***. Follow him at @jksnotkidding on Instagram or @JKLarkinTM on Facebook to keep up to date with his artistic journey.

Also from "The Red Penguin Collection"

Realiteen: Reflections On Growing Up

What Lies Beyond: Sci-Fi Stories of the Future

A Trip For The Books

I Can't Find My Flashlight

The Moments

The Beauty Within—Stories of Spirituality, Faith and Love

'Tis The Season—Poems to Lift Your Holiday Spirits

We Made It!—Essays Reflecting On The New Year

www.ingramcontent.com/pod-product-compliance
Lightning Source LLC
Chambersburg PA
CBHW070636310726
48982CB00001B/296

9781637770146